HISTORIOGRAPHY
A History of Historical Writing

By the Same Author

1. Personal and Geographical Names in the Gupta Inscriptions
2. Political History of Imperial Guptas
3. Research Methodology in History
4. इतिहास में शोध विधि

About the Author

Tej Ram Sharma is a Professor in the Department of History, University of Hyderabad. He has served the university for over two decades in various capacities such as Head of the History Department, Dean, School of Social Sciences, and the Member of the Executive Council. Also, Prof. Sharma has been the Co-ordinator of SAP-II, DSA-UGC, Department of History, University of Hyderabad.

Prof. Sharma has participated, organized and chaired many conferences and seminars of interdisciplinary nature. He has won wide acclaim for his earlier works. He has also won many prestigious awards.

HISTORIOGRAPHY
A History of Historical Writing

TEJ RAM SHARMA

CONCEPT PUBLISHING COMPANY, NEW DELHI-110059

Cataloging in Publication Data—DK
Courtesy: D.K. Agencies (P) Ltd. <docinfo@dkagencies.com>

Sharma, Tej Ram, 1941-
Historiography : a history of historical writing/ Tej Ram Sharma.
p. cm.
Includes bibliographical references (p.)
Includes index.
ISBN 81-8069-155-1
ISBN 81-8069-158-6 (pbk.)

1. Historiography. I. Title.

DDC 907.2 21

The views and options expressed in this book are those of the authors and do not neccessarily reflect the views of the organizations to which they belong.

ISBN 81-8069-158-6 (PB)

First Published 2005

Published and Printed by
Ashok Kumar Mittal
Concept Publishing Company
A/15-16, Commercial Block, Mohan Garden
NEW DELHI-110059 (India)

Phones : 25351460, 25351794
Fax : +91-11-25357103
Email : publishing@conceptpub.com

DEDICATED
TO
THE SACRED MEMORY OF THE RENOWNED
ADVOCATE
SHRI SHANKAR RAO BILOLIKAR AND
MRS. S.R. BILOLIKAR
OF HYDERABAD

PREFACE

The present work aims at tracing the evolution of historical thought with a special emphasis on recent historiography. The histories of the human race do not form a single 'story': what they offer are various domains of difference, different ways of being human persons and different forms of culture and social life which do not form the branches of a single developmental tree. Historiography is not alone in this. "Anthropology and psycho-analysis offer other and equally powerful registers of difference, not merely the difference of the exotic, but in psychoanalysis the knowledge that we are not a simple undivided something that we are not at one with ourselves". We need not frown upon the earlier historical writings as we find so much diversity in the concept and craft of history which has been different from country to country as well from time to time that we cannot call any country an epi-centre of history. This shows the diversity of civilizations and cultures in vogue from time to time and place to place in its understanding and writing of history. Each age had its different concept of history, which reflects on the national consciousness, and the spirit of the age in question. Each country had its pattern of history writing and each country exhibited its concern with the kind of subject matter and tradition with which it got involved from time to time. Hence, we are dividing our monograph into three broad categories:

1. Historical writings in the Ancient Period
2. Historical writings in Middle Ages
3. The Modern Historiography – Approaches and Trends.

In Part II while dealing with the Approaches to History the following topics are covered :

1. Nature and Interpretation of History

2. Developments in Historiography During the 19th and 20th Centuries
3. 20th Century Historiography
4. Ethological or Socio-biological View of History
5. Nationalist Approach to History
6. Marxism and Historical Writing
7. Subaltern Historiography
8. Women's History
9. The Annales Tradition – French School of Historians
10. Psychoanalysis and History
11. Oral History
12. Text Books
13. American Historiography During the 19th and 20th Centuries
14. Communal Approach to History
15. Local and Regional Approach to History
16. Historiophoty.

The study will scan the origin and development of the craft through different epochs and conclude on the main trends visible in modern historiography. We shall see that there has been unity and variety within the different schools of historiography in the modern world. What has been projected as post-modern thought or post-modernism in history has been reflected in Jainology or Jain philosophy of *'anekantavada'* the theory of many-sidedness. It argues that all objects of the world are multiform and that they are endowed with infinite qualities and relations. This relative pluralism can be considered from different points of view or *nayas* that show all understanding and judgements as relative and probable. It is further exemplified in *Syadavada* ('syad' meaning 'may be') the theory of conditional prediction, which may be called 'maybeism' or 'perhapsism'. "The Jain dialectic is neither nihilistic nor metaphysical; it is realistic in the sense it accepts the manifoldness of reality and postulates a 'multiverse' as opposed to the concept of a 'universe'...What we have in Jainology is actually 'post-modernist' thinking handed down from ancient India", which needs to be projected and thus this intellectual aspect of Jainology needs to be internationally recognized. However, in view of the complexity of historiography during the 19th and 20th centuries, we plan to devote separate volume for it.

Tej Raj Sharma

REFERENCES

1. Paul Q. Hirst, *Marxism and Historical Writing,* pp. 26-27.
2. N. Krishnaswamy, "Jainology Pre-figured Post-modern Thought", *The Times of India,* Hyderabad, May 8, 2001, p.12.

ACKNOWLEDGEMENTS

The present work is the result of encouragement meted out by my students and friends, after encouraging reception of the book "Research Methodology in History" authored by me and published by Shri Ashok Kumar Mittal of Concept Publishing Company, New Delhi in 2001 that has a paperback edition as well as the Hindi Translation has been printed. My students and friends including Shri Ashok Kumar Mittal exhorted me to write a book on *History of Historical Writing* for which no single book is available and the relevant material is scattered here and there.

The University Authorities, University of Hyderabad were kind enough to grant me a sabbatical leave, which gave me a free time to read, think over and do justice to the subject.

I have collected the relevant material from various authors to whom I feel indebted for the help taken from their works for which they had taken pains for in-depth studies at grassroots level. Here and there I have made my reflections on their works while dealing with this vast variety of sources and material. The purpose of work will be greatly served if it can help the readers in general and students in particular.

I feel indebted to my wife Mrs. Brij Kishori Sharma for her help in so many ways. I also acknowledge the contribution made by my daughter Miss Richa Sharma and my son Mr. Ranjan Sharma for computing the manuscript.

In the end I thank Shri Ashok Kumar Mittal of Concept Publishing Company, New Delhi for speedy and nice production of the work..

T.R. Sharma

CONTENTS

PART – I

HISTORY OF HISTORICAL WRITINGS

1

HISTORICAL WRITINGS IN THE ANCIENT WORLD

The use of the term history here we take in two senses; one, what happened in the past and the second, how it got recorded that time, i.e. it deals with the concept and craft both at the same time. It is stated that history might have started originally even as oral history, regional or local in character in the garb of "tales of a grandfather". Some content of these local tales may get the accretion of legendary matter, being captured into a great theme by some masterminded, would be organized into the epic, which might be associated with a combination of tribes. In course of time, the epic, which might achieve great artistry and would be transmitted through professional storytellers, represented their actual history – sometimes the only history the people knew beyond the time of their grandfathers. In some ways the epic seems to have assisted the transition to what we regard as "genuine history".[1]

We may state that as soon as man started leading a stable life, got settled at one place rather than a leading a mobile nomadic life, i.e. when he achieved the status of a civilization, he began recording the most important happenings in some form or other. By this time they had learnt the art of writing. The kings of Egypt, of Babylonia and Assyria, and of the Hittites and the persons all sought to preserve their glorious deeds for posterity in monumental inscriptions. The more important rulers also accumulated large archives, including both ordinary administrative documents and records specially commemorating their achievements. Some 20,000 clay tablets remain from the collections written for Ashurbanipal of Assyria (668-627 B.C). Both in Egypt and in Babylonia lists of kings were kept in temples, and these were sometimes supplemented by brief annals recording the principal events, though the hatred felt by certain rulers for their predecessors led to periodic destructions of older material. The exceptional meagreness of the narrative sources for Babylonian history before 747 B.C. seems due to obliteration of the older annals by Nabonassar of Babylonia (ruled 747-734 B.C.). This tradition continued for a period of more than 1,000 years with some changes in literary style. However, it is not possible to get true information about particular events nor we find the material being used to write continuous histories.[2] We find the primary concern of historiography in compiling the Dynastic lists or genealogies, before they become interested in the historical enquiry, or aware of the possibilities. In Sumer and Egypt we find such tremendous lists, however it becomes difficult to identity the rulers. An annual measurement of the flooding of the Nile was recorded in Egyptian annals. An official list of events was kept in Babylonia, in the first Babylonian empire the years were not numbered; they were named after the events. After Babylonia had first established an empire, there appeared the first interpretation of history, based on the very ancient view that disaster fell on any state, which neglected its gods. In Mesopotamia we find the earliest pieces of narration that survive in the form of boundary stones where the story is told as establishing the rights of the case and rehearsing the precedents. We may mention that a Hittite monarch explained a policy decision, provided a retrospective account, which ran through a number of reigns and Hittite treaties are remarkable for the very considerable account they give of the origin of wars. The Hittite annals would seem to have been the most distinguished, whether as history or as historical explanation, and though deeply religious, coming close in this respect to the ancient Hebrews, they bring us surprisingly near to ancient Greece as well. Ancient Hebrews showed powerful narrative gifts and were the first to produce anything like a national history – the first to sketch out the history of mankind from the time of creation.[3]

HISTORIOGRAPHY OF THE ANCIENT GREEKS AND ROMANS

It is in comparison to the above historiography, the inscriptions and temple records, which were normally intended to perpetuate the glory of the gods in whose service these rulers had accomplished great deeds that Herodotus distinguishes himself, who has been called as 'the father of history' by the Roman statesman Cicero. Herodotus came from the Western coast of Asia Minor and was preceded by mainly Ionians from the Greek settlements in the same area. The origin of the Greek historiography lies in the Ionian thought of the 6th century. He introduced his work as an "inquiry" (historia). History is a Greek word meaning simply an investigation or inquiry. Herodotus, who uses in the title of his work, thereby 'marks a literary revolution (as croiset, an historian of Greek literature, says')[4]. Previous writers had been writers down of current stories : the historians say 'How and Wells, sets out to "find" the truth'. It is the use of this word, and its implications, that make Herodotus, the father of history. Out of the four characteristics of history set out by Collingwood, the first, second and fourth of these characteristics clearly appear in Herodotus:

> (a) that it is scientific or begins by asking questions, (b) that it is humanistic, or asks questions about things done by men at determinate times in the past; (d) that it is self-revelatory, or exists in order to tell man what man is by telling him what man has done. It is clear that history for Herodotus is humanistic as distinct from either mythical or theocratic. It ministers to man's knowledge of man; Herodotus sees events as actions of human beings who had reasons for acting as they did. Herodotus makes no mention of evidence (the third of the characteristics mentioned by Collingwood). Thucydides satisfies all the four criteria fixed by Collingwood including the third one, i.e. evidence as he does say explicitly that historical enquiry rests on evidence. 'When I consider in the light of evidence.' He defends his choice of subject by saying that events earlier than those of Peloponnesian War cannot be accurately ascertained.[5] Greek thought worked out a distinction between two types of thought: 'knowledge proper' and 'opinion'. Opinion is empirical semi-knowledge. We have of matters of fact, which are always changing. The Greek identified historical with the reports of the facts given by eyewitnesses of those facts. Evidence consists of eyewitnesses' narratives and

historical method consists of eliciting these.[6] Herodotus makes no specific mention of his evidence; we have to guess it while Thucydides explicitly clarifies it. The Greek conception of history was non-deterministic because the Greeks regarded the cause of history, as flexible and open to salutary modification by the well-instructed human will. Nothing that happens is inevitable. "The person who is about to be involved in a tragedy is actually overwhelmed by it only because he is too blind to see his danger. If he saw it, he could guard against it. Thus the Greeks had a lively and indeed a naïve sense of the power of man to control his own destiny, and thought of this power as limited only by the limitations of his knowledge."[7] The work of Herodotus or Thucydides depends in the main on the testimony of eyewitnesses with whom the historian had personal contact. "Herodotus may be the father of history, but Thucydides is the father of psychological history as he had been largely influenced by Hippocrates who was not only the father of medicine but also was the father of psychology. Thucydides introduced the method of speeches, which seems to be his own comments upon the acts of the speakers, reconstructions of their motives and intentions.[8]

Roman Historians

The idea of world-history was still non-existent as the only genuinely historical method hitherto 'invented by the Greeks was dependent on cross-questioning eyewitnesses; consequently the backward limit of any historian's field was dictated by the limits of human memory. Polybius had taken up to throw light on the conquest of the world by Rome. His ability to do this is connected with the fact that he is working in Rome, whose people had a kind of historical consciousness quite different from that of the Greeks. "History, for him, is worth-studying not because it is scientifically true or demonstrative, but because it is a school and training ground for political life."[9] Polybius does not think that the study of history will enable men to avoid the mistakes of their predecessors and surpass them in worldly success; the success to which the study of history can lead is for him an inner success, a victory not over the circumstances but over self. Man can no longer achieve victory over his fate. What he tries to do succeeds or fails in proportion to his own intelligence or lack of it; the freedom of his will is shown not in controlling the outward events of his life but in controlling the inward temper in which he faces these events.[10] Generally the Greek wrote on contemporary events. Herodotus wrote on the Persian war; Thucydides wrote on the Peloponnesian war while Polybius wrote on the Punic wars.

Herodotus (480-430 B.C.) wrote history partly in order that great deeds (whether of Greeks or non-Greeks) should be placed on record and partly because he wished to levy out the causes of the Greco-Persian war. He looked for the causes of the war, showing the influence of climate and geographical factors and presenting excellent portrayal of character and his feeling for the role of the city in the Persian War. Thucydides while analysing the cause of Peloponnesian war was influenced by the science of the time and tried to apply the principles and methods of Hippocratic medicine to politics, so that everything could be covered by rational explanation. He could separate the immediate occasion from the deeper causes of an event, and was able to proceed to general conclusions connecting it to Athenian imperialism. He realized that something like 'contemporary' history was feasible and he made uses of speeches to communicate what we should regard as the historian's explanations of facts or situations, or of the motives and ideas behind human actions.[11] Polybius was against the "dramatizing" methods that had become popular among historical writers. He traces the rise of Rome and particularly its development to World Empire. He is unable to find out the causes and effects and their inter-connections in the whole network of events, or to discern general tendencies and he shows the operation of chance, the role of unexpected, as part of the very constitution of history.[12] Polybius has been praised by Brown stating that he wrote to instruct, not to entertain. Polybius believed in the eminent significance of the individual in history. He dissected character but criticized the inclusion of needless biographical detail. He thought deeply about individual and mass psychology, and about national character and its relationships to the physical and institutional environment. Polybius was remarkably impartial in his allocation of both praise and blame, for he found the character of individuals to be inconsistent, changing according to circumstances and over time.[13] Methodology, Polybius relied more on oral sources and observation than on documents.[14]

With Polybius the Hellenistic tradition of historical thought passes into the hands of Rome. Livy tookover the gigantic task of assembling the traditional records of early Roman history and welds them together into a single continuous narrative, the history of Rome. It was the first time anything of the sort had been done. It took the form of universal history, the history of the only genuinely historical reality: Oecumenical history, "because Rome had now, like Alexander's empire, become the world".[15] Livy emphasized the role of tradition and accepted to repeat it in good faith. Historians never took up Livy's task again; either copied him and confined themselves to a narrative of recent past. According to Collingwood Tacitus represents a decline, with the remarks that history cannot be scientifically written unless the historian can re-enact in his own mind the experience of the people whose actions he is narrating. Tacitus never tried to do this: his characters are seen not from inside, with understanding and sympathy, but from outside, as never spectacles of virtue or vice. His character drawing is an outrage on historical truth.[16] Subsequent historians made no improvement on it and contented themselves with the wretched business of compilation.[17]

Chief Features of Greco-Roman Historiography

We may sum up the character of Greco-Roman historiography as follows:

Humanism

It is a narrative of human history, the history of man's deeds, man's purposes, man's successes and failures. It admits the role of divine agency, which is strictly limited. The gods have no plan of their own for in the development of human affairs; they only grant success or decree failure for the plans of man. "This implies that whatever happens in history happens as a direct result of human will; that someone is directly responsible for it, to be praised or blamed as it is a good thing or a bad.[18] Collingwood, however, does not bury the idea of accuracy or definiteness of human action with a clear end stating "most human action is tentative, experimental, directed not by a knowledge of what it will lead to but rather by a desire to know what will come of it."[19]

Collingwood considers humanism, however weak as the chief merit of Greco-Roman historiography and states substantialism as its chief defect. It is constructed on the basis of a metaphysical system whose chief category is the category of substance. The events can be known but agent cannot be known to historian. It is taken for granted that the historian's proper business is with acts, which come into being in time, develop in time through their phases, and terminate in time. The agent from which they flow, being a substance is eternal and unchanging and consequently stands outside history. For example as quoted by Collingwood, Livy while attempting the task of writing a history of Rome never took up the task of finding out the process which brought into existence the characteristic Roman institutions and moulded the typical Roman character. Though Rome is the agent whose actions he is describing what people and things do, the nature of these people and things remaining outside its field of vision. The events remain as mere transitory accidents, were regarded as unknowable indeed, but not to the historian. But what then was the use of history? It produces a kind of defeatism about historical accuracy. Collingwood criticises Tacitus for misrepresenting facts by hypocritically concealing the true nature of his characters. Features in the character of Tiberius (whose character broke down beneath the strain of empire) or a Nero[20] which only appeared comparatively late in life must have been these all the time. A good man cannot become bad. A man who shows himself bad when old must have been equally bad when young, his vices concealed by hypocrisy. As the Greeks put it: Power does not alter a man's character; it only shows what kind of man he already was. "Greco-Roman historiography can therefore never show how anything comes into existence; all agencies that appear on the stage of history have to be assumed readymade before history begins, and they are related to historical events exactly as a machine is related to its own movements."[21]

Tacitus was quite aware of the difference between people's motives and their statements and between their statements and their actions. He was very good at seeing the complexity of things and was impartial in praise and blame. Among the sources Tacitus consulted were memoirs, earlier historians, probably the *acta senatus* (a daily gazette that had been instituted by Julius Caesar) biographies, autobiographies, occasional inscriptions and some oral sources. He was critical of his sources, though he sometimes relied on only a few sources when more were available and rarely can be caught in a falsehood.[22] Tacitus even achieved a sense of comparative historiography, noting: "The subject matter of history varies according as the constitution about which the historian writes is democracy, oligarchy or monarchy.[23] Brown concludes that in spite of these strengths, Tacitus was not much read in Rome, because pragmatic or serious history "became unfashionable, giving way to imperial biography and panegyric"[24]. A decline in Roman historiography has been accepted virtually by all authorities with a few exceptions. Tacitus has been praised for his character-drawing but has been equally blamed for a rigid description of personal character of a historical figure withput any impact of environment on it.[25] Afterwards the historians began to content themselves uncritically with the task of compilation of material from the earlier works rather than improving upon defects of the writings of Livy and Tacitus.[26]

THE INFLUENCE OF CHRISTIANITY ON HISTORICAL WRITING

The progress in the development of European historio-graphy was retarded in someway by the influence of Christianity. Collingwood[27] states that it jettisoned two of the leading ideas in Greco-Roman historiography : (i) The optimistic idea of human nature and (ii) The substantialistic idea of eternal entities underlying the process of historical change.

According to Christian view human action is not designed in view of preconceived ends by the intellect, it is actuated *a tergo* by immediate and blind desire. The achievements of man are not due to his own proper forces of will and intellect but to something other than himself, causing him to desire ends that he pursues. The wisdom displayed in his action is not his; it is the wisdom of God, by whose grace man achieves his ends.

The metaphysical doctrine of substance in Greco-Roman philosophy was challenged by the Christian doctrine of creation. "Nothing is eternal except God, and all else has been created by god; each soul is believed to be a fresh creation – peoples and nations substances but have been created by God. And what God has created. He can modify by a reorientation of its nature towards fresh ends, thus by the operation of His grace."[28] It had a three-fold effect on historiography:

(1) Historical process is the working out not of man's purposes but of God's: God's purpose being a purpose for man. God is the motivator of all human actions – whatever happens in history happens by his will. This thinking brought in the role of providence in view.

(2) The human beings as agents serve as vehicles of God's purposes and are therefore historically important.

(3) It brought out the idea of universality. All persons and all peoples are involved in the working out of God's purpose, and therefore the historical process is everywhere and always of the same kind. And every part of it is a part of the same whole. It conceived of history of the world, a universal history whose theme shall be the general development of God's purposes for human life and not any other partial and particularistic history.

"The infusion of Christian ideas overcomes not only the characteristic humanism and the substantialism of Greco-Roman history, but also its particularism."[29] Collingwood further remarks that any history written on Christian principles will be of necessity – universal, providential, apocalyptic, and periodized. It will be a universal history, or history of the world, going back to the origin of man. It will describe how the various races of men came into existence and peopled the various habitable parts of the earth. It will describe the rise and fall of civilizations and powers. Greco-Roman occu-menical history is not universal in this sense, because it has particularistic centre of gravity. Greece or Rome is the centre round which it revolves."[30]

The triumph of Christianity in the Roman Empire during the fourth century assured the predominance of the type of historiography radically different from the historians of the Pagan Greek and Roman historians. Its origin were Jewish. The Jews were the only people of antiquity who had the supreme religious duty of remembering the past because their traditional histories commemorated the working out of God's plan for his chosen people. By contrast, no Greek even heard his gods ordering him to remember. The Jewish sacred writings were ultimately gathered into what became the Old Testament. They were only concerned with the selection of such facts as seemed relevant in interpreting god's purpose. The Christians took over the Old Testament and added to an additional body of sacred history. The writers of the four gospels included in the New Testament were bearing witness to assured truths that the faithful ought to know, and no convincing reconstruction of historical facts is possible from these books of the New Testament. The New Testament as a whole represents merely a selection from the early Christian writings.[31]

Christian history has to be a universal history, though of a very peculiar sort, where only one sequence of privileged events, Jewish and Christian, deserved detailed record. The early Christians were forced to fit some pagan history into their universal scheme. This was achieved by means of universal chronologies from the creation of the world to each writer's own time. The events of Jewish and Christian history were thus synchronized with the main dates of the Pagan myth and history. Sextus Julius Africanus (early 3rd century), the first Christian writer allotted 6,000 years to the whole span of human history and placed the birth of Christ in the year 5500 from the creation of the world. This work provided the model for the more elaborate *Chronographia* (Chronicle) of Eusebius. Dionysius Exiguris, who wrote at Rome in the early 6th century, introduced the dating from the birth of Christ and the English historians successfully popularized it in the 8th century. Bede Eusebius was the earliest and most important of Christian historians of the

4th century. He wrote Ecclesiastical history designed to show how, through a long series of acts of Divine Providence, a Christian empire was finally brought into existence by Constantine.

Biography was adapted to Christian purposes. St. Jerome compiled the lives of 135 Christian writers. St. Augustine in his 'City of God' showed his vision of the divine and the earthly cities confronting each other dominated the outlook of all the medieval Christian thinkers and profoundly affected their treatment of history. Within that divine plan for the world, purely secular history seemed an insignificant thing.[32]

A central importance was attached to the historical life of the Christ. It will divide history into two parts, each having a peculiar and unique character of its own: first, a forward-looking character, consisting in blind preparation for an event yet not revealed, second, a backward looking character depending on the fact that the revelation has now been made. A history thus divided into two periods, a period of darkness and a period of light, which Collingwood calls *apocalyptic* history[33]. "The apocalyptic idea became a commonplace, although historians have placed their apocalyptic moment at all sorts of time; the Renaissance, the invention of printing, the scientific movement of the seventeenth century, the enlightenment of the eighteenth, the French revolution, the Liberal movement of the nineteenth century, or even, as with Marxist historians, in the future"[34] further remarks Collingwood.

EAST ASIAN HISTORIOGRAPHY
(Historiography in China)

History was the "Queen of the Sciences" for the Chinese. The historical writing in China goes as far back as 1000 B.C. – for the instruction of the ruler. Some scholars like Van der Loon who says that the clear evidence comes somewhat later, i.e. 700 B.C. when the early scribes, with ritual or divinatory functions provided the idea of chronology and that by about 400 B.C., a conscious historical tradition had emerged. Historical writing from this early period was concerned with statecraft. Beginning in the eighth century B.C., the Chou dynasty gradually disintegrated and a series of lesser states emerged, each keeping its own archival records. The chronicle of one of these states was edited by Confucius (552-479 B.C.), and has been preserved under the name of the *Spring and Autumn Annals*. Confucius was more interested in practical politics: he sought to show the rewards of virtue and the dangers of evil.[35] However, an unknown compiler around the end of the fourth century B.C., had prepared another chronicle from the archives of three other states, and portions of this chronicle were subsequently appended to the *Spring and Autumn Annals*, which inform us about China's "feudal periods". The father and son Ssu-ma Tan and Ssu-ma Chein (*c.*145-85 B.C.), court astrologers wrote the *Records of the historians* which is stated to be "the first general history of china". Out of the two the son Ssu-ma Chein is regarded as the founder of Chinese historiography striking similarity to that of the historians of his approach shows a ancient Greece and Rome.[36] His "objective detachment" enabled him even to criticize his own emperor, as he believed in the educative nature of history. Thus he set a standard copied for centuries by official historians. When the *History of the former Han Dynasty*, the first of the "standard histories" was written, it copied the *Records of the Historian*, dropping only the section on local ruling houses. The diaries, which grew out of the record of astrologers, may have been heft from as early as the Chou Dynasty (1050-249 B.C.) but at any rate were consulted for writing the official history of the later Han dynasty (A.D. 25-220). In the later Han the work of astrologers came to an end, and scholars were appointed as official historians. Later, in T'ang times (7th century A.D.), the bureau of historiography was established and it lasted until 1911. Both modern China, as well as such agencies as the party and the army, have reinstituted bureaus of historiography. Towards the end of the later Han Dynasty an official history, the *Han chi*, was composed, commissioned by the emperor, by Hsuan Yueh (A.D.148-209). Hsuan's comments were made on earlier Han, but it was clear that the lessons he drew were applicable to later Han as well. Hsuan later wrote the *Shen-Chien* (Extended Reflections); so his *Chien* (mirror) stimulated many similar works.[37] In the third century, history had been established as a distant branch of learning, and in the fourth century, schools of history were established in both the northern and southern dynasties. Chinese historians from Ssu-ma Chien onward commented at least sporadically on their own work, Liu Chih-Chi (A.D. 661-72) was first to write a treatise on historiography, possibly the first such work in any language. Liu set forth three standards for rejecting materials: internal inconsistency, inconsistency with more reliable sources and inherent impossibility. He criticized Ssu-me Chien for employing a supernatural explanation of the fall of a state. "When one discusses the rise and fall of states one ought certainly to take human affairs as the essential; if one must bring fate into one's discourse then reason is outraged." He criticized "the deliberate twisting or concealment" as the principal source of error in historical materials as well as criticized the use of high flown language in the fictitious speeches of persons unlikely to use such language.[38]

After Liu-Chih-Chi, the next major historiographical advance was made by Ssu-ma Kuang who lived in the eleventh century during the Northern Sung Dynasty this *Comprehensive Mirror for Aid in Government* chronicled Chinese history from 403 B.C. to A.D. 959 and achieved a stature alongside of Ssu-ma Chien's *Records of the Historian*. Ssu-ma Kuang was certainly a scientific historian as he insisted on reasons being explicitly given.[39] For example, he after describing a certain set of factions, goes on to provide a short treatise on the "causes and effects of bureaucratic factionalism."[40] Chinese believed that history teaches lessons. Mostly the lessons were moral called as "moral didacticism", which got extended to historical analogism. It has been pointed out that Chinese had no system of formal logic; hence they could not develop "the habit of framing generalizations in a hypothetical-deductive form".[41]

"During the several centuries when historical analogism pushed moral didacticism into the background, government into the background, government patronage was an important factor. From eighth to thirteenth century, historical problems were standard elements in bureaucratic examinations, and historians played an important role in the education of a ruler. A substantial portion of the "policy questions" in the imperial examinations "required the examinee to use historical models in proposing solutions to contemporary problems. The education of the emperor had long been a matter of great concern, but the establishment in 1033 of the "Imperial Seminar" in which the ruling emperor participated, gave historians direct access to the emperor and influence over policy decisions. In the Sung Dynasty (960-1279) an "Imperial Policy Chronicle" represented "the most ambitious attempt to adapt historical writing to the needs of policy-makers." We quote from Hartwell in this context as follows: "From eighth to thirteenth century, emperors, statesmen, and historians avowed that history provides the means to understand the success and failure of different forms of governmental organization, the rise and fall of dynasties, the evolution and transformation of laws and institutions, the advantage and injury resulting from specific measures, and the nature of human behaviour."[42] Actually as stated from the seventh century under the T'ung Dynasty, there had emerged a history office, which was an organ of government, and history became an important subject in civil service examination, which now achieved its permanent form as a competitive affair – a high proportion of government officials would spend part of their careers in History Bureau, and historical narratives came to be produced on the committee method. *The Diaries of Activity and Response* reproduced the utterances of the Emperor and the business that he conducted, day by day. These were abridged to that when the Emperor died, there emerged a *Veritable Record*, a survey of the whole reign. When a dynasty came to an end, a comprehensive account would be written under the succeeding dynasty; and this, the *Standard History* was an important thing, produced for nearly two thousand years on a pattern set initially in the first century A.D. by Pan Ku in his *History of the Former Han Dynasty*.[43] No nation possesses such voluminous, continuous and (within their own terms) accurate records of so long past. "It was all official history, written by civil servants for civil servants and not intended to form reading matter for wider public. Even those who wrote history privately would themselves belong to the official class and would need government records – they might be aspiring to enter the civil service."[44]

"While in China the archivist-astrologer-recorder sometimes acquired great influence at the imperial court and acted as secretary to the ruler or went on diplomatic missions. He descends from the "temple-archivist" who in the place where sacrifices were made to ancestors, looked after the documents – the registers, inventories, family trees, records of contracts, and decisions of the oracles. In case of princely houses, he would draw up treaties, record edicts and draft documents, which granted feudal enfeoffment. But also he had charge of divination and would decide the day for making a journey, holding a ceremony, beginning a war. From an early date the archivist-astrologer recorded events, and in this he was perhaps regarded as making a report to ancestral spirits. He would also look after the calendar, recorded eclipses of the Sun and Moon, and deal with the time-table generally."[45]

"In India there was a professional class of historians or chroniclers called the Sutas, the Magadhas also called Bhrigvangirasas who assembled the chronologies of the Royal Dynasty in Chronological order. Whether they enjoyed some kind of royal patronage but they were not in the service (as in China) of the king."[46] Moreover the chronicle had one serious shortcoming that they did not develop any formal system of logic,[47] hence a Chinese historian was not supposed to be an interpreter,[48] while Indians had a well-developed system of logic called *Tarka-Shastra* or *Nyaya Shastra*.

In the 17th century a remarkable group of historical scholars virtually founded a school of critical Chinese philosophy. "None of these writers succeeded in radically transforming Chinese historiography, but they created an increasingly sophisticated and critical tradition. Their successors in the 20th century assimilated some valuable features of modern Western historiography."[49]

INDIAN HISTORIOGRAPHY: HISTORIOGRAPHY IN ANCIENT INDIA

It is quite strange and regrettable that some foreign authors charge Indian historiography with absence or meagreness of genre of history before the advent of Islam while showering high praise for Greco-Roman, Chinese, Christian or Muslim historiography.[50] This is not true, as "Every society can be called a-historical".[51] This does not mean that ancient Indians developed the art of history like others quoted above but attempts were made from time to time to write the chronicle of a particular reign or dynasty. "There are indications that the ancient Indians did not lack historical sense. This is proved by the carefully preserved list of teachers in various Vedic texts, as well as in the writings of the Buddhists, Jains and other religious texts. Even as late as seventh century A.D., Hiuen Tsang noticed that each province in India had its own official for maintaining written records of good and evil events, calamities and fortunate occurrences. It is necessary to point out that ever since the time of Samudragupta, Indian kings were want to have the chronicles of their dynasties and victories written by some famous poet on stone. The last noteworthy example of this type of literature is the large inscription set-up by Rana Kumbhakarna of Mewar".[52] During the period from several centuries B.C. until the fourth century A.D., some of the materials in the form of the *puranas* were compiled and ultimately written down since they were compiled and maintained by specialists (the Sutas and the Magadhas) they should be considered accurate because we have no reason to believe that specialists would systematically memorise false-hoods.[53] Pathak cites the example of biographies to make an effort to get inside the minds of their authors by the historian to glean facts from these accounts.[54] Their importance as a genre related to history cannot be set aside by sundry remarks that they "cannot be considered as history in anything like the modern sense"[55]. "To this extent, the form in which a sense of history was expressed in ancient India must be judged by the literature of other ancient classical cultures".[56] "What is perhaps more important is to try and understand what was regarded as relevant and why",[57] says Romila Thapar.

Warder has made an intensive study of Indian historiography and is of the opinion that "there exists a vast amount of historical writing of various kinds in the Indian tradition contrary to generally received opinion".[58] He has also thrown ample light on the historiography which itself becomes regional during the medieval period.[59] Apart from Hindu, Buddhist and Jaina historiography[60], Warder has dealt with extensively the regional historiography which started with seventh century and consumed till modern times, viz. Chalukya and Rashtrakuta historiography, Pala historiography, historiography in Kashmir, Sindhu and Gurjara, Jejakabhukti, Kamarupa, Kerala, Hoyasala, Andhra, Kalinga and Maharashtra.[61]

Monier-Williams defines Itihasa (Iti-ha-as) so indeed it was – talk, legend, tradition, history, traditional accounts of former events, heroic history on the basis of *Satapatha Brahmana*, the *Mahabharata*, and the *Manusmrti*.[62] The earliest Vedic text is the *Rgvedasamhita* – a large collection composed probably between 1500 and 1000 B.C. It is a Brahminical ritual text but consists of collection of songs and prayers and books of ritual and speculation. It contains references to contemporary historical text and some historical pieces have been incorporated in the *Veda*. It is basically a religious canon and the independent historical texts have been preserved in their original form. They may be partly preserved in the extant *Itihasa* codified in a later period. We may mention the *Indragathis*, poems on the deeds of Indra, the War god. Some *gathas* are distinguished as *narasamsi,* 'in praise of man'. The poem called the Ten Kings (Dasarajna) praises the Brahmin minister Vasistha who guided his king Sudas to victory the Ten. In the Vedic literature there are also *akhyanas,* 'narratives' – 'histories' or 'epics' often in prose but sometimes in verse or in a mixture of both (e.g. on the 'Flood', *Satapathabrahmana* 1.8.1). The term *akhyana* later meant 'epic', as in case of the *Mahabharata*. The *paripalavani* (cycle) was an *akhyana* on a series of great emperors to be recited during the year leading up to a horse-sacrifice.[63]

Later Vedic texts, the *Atharvaveda Samhita*, *Satapatha-brahmana*, *Chandogyopanisad* and others refer to *Itihasa* 'tradition' or 'history' as branches of literature or as another *Veda* or *Vedas*. The original *Purana* seems to have been a single text, which collected the narratives and genealogies of ancient kings from various old sources and arranged and connected them in chronological sequence. The composer in the 8th century B.C. was Lomaharsana or alternatively he received it from 'Vyasa'[64] (or Krsna Dvaipayana), who should have lived a century earlier. According to the information given by Alberuni (A.D. 1030) "Krsna Dvaipayana is Vyasa, the son of Parasara. The twenty-ninth Vyasa has not yet come, but will appear in future."[65]

We are reminded of the famous Sanskrit saying *"Itihasa-puranabhayam Vedam Upabrimhyet"* – 'Veda should be elaborated with the help of Itihasa and Purana'. In later times, at least *Itihasa* is the more general term and embraces all the old historical and related traditions, including the *Puranas*. "As *Itihasa* outside the *Purana* we have the traditions of the *Bharata Akhayana* (extant in its later form the *Mahabharata*), narrating the events of a great civil war in the Bharata or Kaurava Dynasty (which took place between about 950 and 900 B.C which Rao has fixed it as 1500 B.C. on the basis of Dwarka excavations) and attributed to the same 'Vyasa'. In its extent from this epic incorporates many other *akhyanas* such as the *Yayataka* (story of emperor Yayati) and such narrations outside a genealogical *framework* or chronological framework may have been what was originally understood by *Itihasa* as distinct from *purana*".[66]

In the Rgveda the cult of sacrifice was given prime importance. In the *Rgveda* X.90[67], the *purusha-sukta*, it is stated the world was first created out of the sacrifice performed by the primeval *purusha.* "Brahmana was his mouth, rajanya the arms, vaisya the thighs and from his feet sudra was produced. The moon was gendered from his mind, and from his eye sun had birth; Indra and Agni from his mouth were born, and vayu from his breath; Forth from his naval came mid-air; the sky was fashioned from his head; Earth from his feet and from his ear the regions. Thus they formed the worlds." We may state that the perception of historical reality differed from age to age. If the cult of sacrifice was the most prime thing of an age, in the succeeding period the doctrine of *dharma* was given the prime importance. It was believed that any calamity in the world is due to violation of *dharma* 'natural order'. We quote from Yaska (7th – 8th century B.C.) who says that now we narrate history *(Itihasa).* In the Kuru country, Rishtishena had two sons Devapi and Shantanu. Shantanu the younger son got himself anointed as king. Devapi went for penance. After that it didn't rain for twelve years in Shantanu's kingdom. The Brahmanas told him "you have acted contrary to *dharma* by ignoring the claim of elder brother you got yourself anointed as king. So the gods do not let rain. Shantanu requested Devapi to get back the kingdom then Devapi retorted, "I will act as your priest and help you to perform sacrifice. In that reference is this *Varshauramasukta*".[68]

Another illustration has been quoted by the poet Bhavabhuti (8th century A.D.) in his *Uttara-ramacharitam* act II. In *Ramarajya* no son should die when his father is alive. Once a reporter brought a news to the contrary for which Lord Rama went himself in search immediately for the transgression of *Dharma*. He found a sudra named Shambuka engaged in deep penance in a forest. Lord Rama killed Shambuka to save his kingdom from further calamities. Shambuka obtained *moksha* (liberation from the circle of life and death) being killed by the lord who was an incarnation of Vishnu. Later even the theory of incarnation revolves around this theme as the Lord Krishna himself (who is an incarnation of Vishnu) told in the *Shrimad Bhagvad Gita,* "Arjuna, whenever there is decline of righteousness and unrighteousness is in the ascendant, then I body myself forth for the protection of the virtuous, for the destruction of the wicked and for establishment of *Dharma* (righteousness) on a firm footing, I'm born from age to age."[69]

Later on to this theory of *Dharma* was added to the theory of *Karma* (action). Any good action is rewarded and any bad action gets punished. Ultimately the truth or good wins forth *(Satyameva Jayate)*. Lord Krishna himself explains in the *Srimad Bhagavad Gita*, "All beings abide in me the whole world is deluded by objects evolved from the three modes of nature – *Sattva, Rajas* and *Tamas,* which is my wonderful *illusion (Maya)*". When Lord Krishna finds Arjuna disillusioned and stranded in the war against his relatives and teachers starts, sermonizing Arjuna to his duty *(Karma)* of a *Kshatriya,* "Therefore, do you arise and win glory, conquering foes, enjoy the affluent kingdom. These warriors are already slain by age; be you only an instrument, Arjuna."[70] We can compare this Indian belief with a similar perception in ancient Mesopotamia and Egyptian civilizations that Lord created the world as his sport (*Lila*) or what we call his *illusion (Maya)* and that acting against the works of Gods is sinful or that God is responsible for rise and fall of civilizations.[71]

According to traditional belief all natural calamities such as pestilence, famines, drought, floods, etc. are interpreted as punishment for evil actions on the part of the people of the state. The war has been interpreted as a fight between the good and the evil, the former representing the gods and the latter the demons. The wars depicted in both the Epics, the *Ramayana* and the *Mahabharata,* between Rama and Ravana and between the Pandavas and the Kauravas, represented fight between the good and the evil in which message conveyed is that whosoever is born on this earth has to go through the trauma of life and death. Even Lord Rama and Krishna were themselves incarnations of Vishnu when born in this world in human form had to bear with the human troubles and had to carry out the responsibilities bestowed on them. We read in the last and the most pregnant *sloka* of *Srimad Bhagvad Gita*[72]; "Whenever there is the combination (*Yoga*) of the divine purpose of Krishna and the indomitable determination and valour of Arjuna, wielder of the *Gandiva* bow, there will surely be the blessings of prosperity, welfare, success and eternal justice for the people in the state."[73]

Indian Literary Tradition of Boon and Curse

The *Karma* theory is a part and parcel of Indian psyche and is connected with the circle of birth and death. People are born again and again to go through their *Karmic* cycle, to bear the fruits of their good and bad actions.

Sri Aurobindo states: "The inevitable logic of causes and results, actions and their fruits which we call *Karma*... The tree must bear its own proper fruit and Nature is always a diligent gardener."[74] Sri Aurobindo blames "the constantly accumulating *Karma* of successful injustice and the violent revolutions are the natural reactions of it. What was in the past will be still sown in the present and continue to return on us in the future."[75]

We may state that during the Epic period, the importance of cult of sacrifice remained in tact. King Dasaratha's four sons were born out of his three queens as a result of a sacrifice (*Yajna*) performed by him with the help of his priest Vasistha and others. As a result Kausalya gave birth to Rama, Bharata was born to Kakeyi and Sumitra gave birth to two sons, Lakshmana and Satrughna. The birth of Rama has been described in the *Valmiki Ramayana* to meet out the boon granted by Brahma, the creator of the world to Ravana. The Indian tradition connects this event as a result of a curse from the parents of Sravana Kumar who had come to a pond and was dropping the vessel in it to fill it with water to quench the thirst of his aged blind parents, mistaken to be a wild animal, King Dasaratha shot an arrow instantaneously killing Sravana Kumar. King Dasaratha then took upon himself to quench the thirst of Sravana Kumar's parents. On questioning his identity, they hurled a curse on King Dasaratha, "You will realise this when you will suffer the pangs of separation of your son". This came true when King Dasaratha had to suffer the similar fate due to seeking of two boons (granted to her by King Dasaratha for her services in war between gods and demons) by Queen Kakeyi who was ill advised by her female servant Manthara when King Dasaratha was going to anoint Lord Rama as the king of Ayodhya as such, "Punishment of Rama to forest for fourteen years and that Bharata be made the ruler of the earth." As a result King Dasaratha had to lament in grief for the separation of his eldest and most beloved son Rama, which ultimately resulted in his death.[76] Even another story is connected with the birth of Lord Rama as an incarnation of Vishnu who had to go through the ordeal of losing Sita by King Ravana of Lanka and was helped by monkey-king Hanumana. This was due to a curse fallen on lord Rama from sage Narada who had once gone to Lord Visnu to grant him a beautiful form with the desire to marry a queen in *svayamvara* ceremony. Instead Lord gave him form of a monkey. Narada beguiled, being assured of his handsomeness walked vainfully into the *svayamvara* when he was stopped with rudeness by the chief doorkeeper and other two guards. And finally one guard let him go in. While not getting the expected response became disillusioned after being shown his face in a pot of water. In a fit of wrath he returned and cursed Lord Vishnu: "You will cry for your wife and this monkey form only will help you." As a result Vishnu had to take birth as Rama and weep for Sita while the main doorkeeper was born as Ravana and the guards as his brothers Kumbhakarna and Meghanatha. The one who had allowed the sage to get into the Svayamvara Pandala was born as Vibhisana.[77]

We also know of Ahalya, wife of Gautama *rshi*, whose story is alluded to in several *Brahmanas* being derived from the epithet of Indra, "Lover of Ahalya". In the *Ramayana* Ahalya had been termed into a stone by the curse of her husband Gautam, charged with infidelity, is stated to have attained *moksha* when the pious feet of Lord Rama touched her.[78]

Indian literary tradition is replete with such examples. In the *Mahabharata* we have the legend of King Sagara who had sixty thousand unworthy sons, who got destroyed by the curse of the sage Kapila whom they annoyed with their misbehaviour while searching for the *Asvamedha* horse in the under world. They were purified by acute penance by their descendant Bhagiratha by bringing Bhagirathi (the Ganges) on the earth.[79]

According to Indian tradition even the first *Kavya*, the *Ramayana* being known as the *Adi-kavya* (first *Kavya*) sprang forth from the heart of Valmiki as a result of suffering from grief after seeing a pair of birds (*Krauncha Mithuna*) who were intertwined with each other out of love and singing sweetly, the male bird being instantaneously killed by the arrow of a cruel hunter and when the female bird, seeing its mate rolling dead on the earth with its limbs besmeared with blood, uttered a plaintive cry – this gave birth to the first *sloka* by the sage in the form of a curse, "O hunter, you shall have no good name for endless years, since you have killed one of the couple of Kraunch birds whilst in the transport of love".[80] This followed the composition of the whole of the *Ramayana* in the *sloka* metrea, divided into four parts, with the same number of syllables in each with rhythm and tone complete.[81]

National poet of Indian culture, Kalidasa, in his famous drama *Abhijanana Sakuntalam* has incorporated the element of curse of the sage Durvasa due to which Dusyanta fails to recognize Sakuntala when she has been sent to him afterwards, which is absent in the original story of the *Mahabharata*,[82] perhaps to provide cover to the deeds of the hero of the play. Even in his lyrical *kavya* the *Meghadutam*, Kalidasa has shown Yaksha cursed by Kubera to be suffering the pangs of separation from his beloved passing the period of his exile of one year at Ramagir Mountain, in the beginning of rainy season addresses the floating clouds to pass on his message to his beloved in Alakapuri.[83]

The *Arthasastra of Kautilya* quotes examples of past rulers who got destroyed owing to curses by the people on whom they inflicted atrocities: The Bhoja king, Dandakya by name, entertaining a sinful desire for a Brahmin maiden, perished along with his kinsmen and kingdom; and (so did) Karala, King of the Videhas. Janamejaya, using violence against Brahmins, out of anger (likewise perished); and so did *Talajanha* (using violence) against the Bhrgus. Aila, extorting money from the four *varnas* out of greed (perished), and so did Ajabindu of Sauviras. Ravana, not restoring the wife of another through pride (perished); and (so did) Duryodhana (not returning) a portion of the kingdom. Dambhodbhava, treating creatures with contempt out of ignorance (perished); and so did Arjuna of the Haihayas. Vatapi, trying to assail Agastya, out of foolhardiness (perished); and so did the clan of the Vrsnis (trying to assail Davipayana)."[84] It seems this tradition was alive even during the times of Alberuni as he talks about the end of Vasudeva. Vasudeva had concerted with Arjuna the arrangement that they would consider the quivering of the left arm or left eye as a mysterious intimation that there was something happening to him. At that time there lived a pious *Rishi* called Durvasas. Now the brothers and relations of Vasudeva were rather malicious, inconsiderate set of people. One of them hid under his coat a new frying pan, went to the anchorite and asked him what would be the result of his pregnancy, jeering at the pious man. The latter said, "In the belly there is something which will be the cause of thy death and that of thy whole clan." When Vasudeva heard this he became sorry because he knew that these words would be fulfilled. He gave orders that the pan should be filed away and be thrown into the water. A fish devoured it; the fish was caught, and the fisherman found it in its belly. He thought it would be a good tip for his arrow.

When the predestined time came, Vasudeva rested on the coast under the shadow of the tree, one of his feet being crossed over the other; the fisherman took him for a gazeele and shot at him and hit his right foot. This wound became the cause of death of Vasudeva.[85] At the same time Arjuna began to quiver and then his arm. Now his brother gave him orders that he should never anymore embrace anybody, that he might not be bereft of his strength (?). Arjuna went to Vasudeva, but could not embrace him on account of his state in which he was. Vasudeva ordered his bow to be brought and handed over to Arjuna, who tried his strength at it. Vasudeva ordered him to burn his body and the bodies of his relations when they had died, and to bring his wives from the castle, and then he died.

Out of the filings or the bits of iron, which had fallen off when the pan had filed a *bardi,* bush had grown. To this there came the Yadavas, who tied together some bundle of its twigs to sit upon. While they were drinking there rose a quarrel between them; they beat each other with *bardi* bundles and killed each other. All this happened near the mouth of river Sarasti, where it flows into the sea, near the situation of Somnath.[86]

Arjuna had done all he had been ordered by Vasudeva. When he brought away the women; robbers suddenly attacked them. Now, when, Arjuna was no longer able to handle his bow, he felt that his strength was going. He whirled the bow in a circle above his head, and all who stood under the bow were saved, while the robbers seized the others. Now Arjuna and his brothers saw that life was no more of any use to them, therefore they emigrated to north and entered the mountains, the snow of which never melts. The cold killed them one after the other, in the end only Yudhisthira remained. He obtained the distinction of being admitted to paradise, but before that he had to pass through hell for the consequence of sole lie he had spoken in his life, at the request of his brothers and Vasudeva these were the words he had spoken within the hearing of Brahmana Drona, "Ashwathama the elephant has died". He had made a pause between Ashwathama and the elephant, by which he led Drona to believe that he meant his son. Yudhisthira spoke to the angels, "If this must be, may my intercession be accepted on behalf of the people in hell; may they be freed from it". After this his desire was granted, he went into paradise.[87] Thus we notice that sage Durvasas' curse and Yudhisthira's deceitful speech had brought forth bad fruits, but Yudhisthira's presence in hell proved to be a boon for the other people in hell because they got freed from it.

We find this element of curse and boon even in the famous *Satyanarayana katha* in the Reva Khanda of the *Skanda Purana* and the folklore of *saptavara-katha* (stories of the seven days) quite popular among the masses.

By the time of Kautilya (*c.*300 B.C.?) the term *Itihasa* had obtained a wider connotation and it covered *purana* stories *Itivrtta* (story, history this might include the *akhyanas* such as *Bharata*), *Akhyayika* (biography such was *Vasavadatta)*. The story of a princess of 5th century B.C., *Udaharana* (illustration, probably short exemplary stories), *dharmasastra* (law) and *arthasastra* (science of government and wealth).[88] Even *Itihasa* was designated as the *Veda*.[89] In the course of time some of the constituent elements of history such as the *Purana*, *Arthasastra* and *Dharmasastra* developed into independent subjects of study. The connotation of *Itihasa* accordingly underwent a great change and was practically narrowed to a record of past events or occurrences. *Itihasa* means past events accompanied by or arranged in the form of stories (*Kathayuktam*) and covering instruction in *Dharma* (morals), *Artha* (wealth), *Kama* (desire) and *Moksha* (salvation), i.e. the four ultimate ends of life.[90]

Indians divided time into four ages (*yugas*) – the *Krta*, *Treta*, *Dvapara* and *Kali*. The first is known as *Satya Yuga* where the *Dharma* stood on the four feet in the form of bull (cf. Manu: *Vrso Bhagwan Dharmah*). Gradually the moral degeneration began – in *Treta* the bull stood on three feet, in *Dvapara* on two feet and finally, degenerated into *Kali-yuga* where the feet of the bull are aloft and quivering. The Bharata war has been taken as having occurred at the close of the *Dvapara* age and the *Kali* age began after the War.[91]

Indians believed in a cyclic concept of history followed by a *Manvantara* each time.[92] This theory, which culminated in the *Puranas,* was known in India as early as the Brahamanic period. The *Satapatha Brahmana* recounts the tale of Manu and the fish connected with the great deluge. Manu once came across a small fish, which requested him to rear it, and promised to save his life from the coming deluge that would inundate the whole universe. According to its suggestion Manu fashioned an ark and boarded the same with the onset of deluge. The ark was finally guided to the northern mountain by the fish, to whose horn the ship was tied. Thus Manu's life was saved and he became the progenitor of mankind.[93]

The *puranas* deal with five topics and are exponents of cyclic theory of time. The five topics, in the definition of *purana – panchalakshana* are *sargas* (the creation of universe); *prati-sarga* (world's destruction and recreation); *vamsa* (the genealogy of the gods and patriarchs); *manvantara* (the regions and periods of the Manus) and *vamsanucharita* (the history of the solar and lunar races of kings).[94]

Earlier the job of compiling the genealogies in the *puranas* was trusted to the *sutas*. Thus Lomaharsana was a *suta*. Some of the sources connect *sutas* with the Bhrgu (i.e. Bhargava), Angiras (Bharadvaja) and Kasyapa clan of priests of whom the first two seem to have been especially associated with historiography (with *Itihasa* and *purana*). However, the warriors and other Aryans (*Vaisyas*) in ancient times took the clan name of their priests, so that it is not necessary to suppose that the *sutas* were Brahmanas. Later the *Magadhas*, a school of Brgivangirs historians belonging to the empire of Magadha gradually revised the *Itihasa* (and as a part of it the *purana*) traditions. The revision of Indian traditions of universal history continued until the 4th century A.D., the intervening dynasties of kings being incorporated in the *Puranas*. The accepted number of these *puranas* is eighteen and equal number is of the *Upa-puranas*, which claim equal antiquity and authority with the 'great' *Puranas* by about the 8th century and their number has doubled since[95]. After this we take notice of many *sthala-puranas,* which are connected, with the religious centres of various regions.

From the 7th century A.D. onwards, the idea of *Itihasa* and *purana* tradition underwent a process of enlargement. It got intensified in the form of various *vamsavalis* or family chronicles maintained in many kingdoms and also gave rise to new genre of historical writing, the historical biography. Romila Thapar explains, it was due to number of reasons. The emergence of small regional kingdoms, based on a feudalistic pattern of functioning, led to the development of local loyalties and interest and a more defined association of a locality with its history. Together with this, the centre of historical interest had moved from the tribe to the king and his court. The heroic tradition had given way to the court and the focus of the court, the king. The *suta* receded into the background and the court poet became central to historical writing.[96] We have numerous inscriptional records available in various scripts which throw a flood of light on various aspects of Indian history through the ages. The inscriptions were of no use to us until James Prinsep deciphered the Brahmi script in 1837 on the analogy of the Kharosthi and Greek inscriptions. From the Asokan inscriptions, we know about his concept of *Dharma,* polity and administration. The Thirteenth Rock Edict informs us about the Kalinga war and his resolve to renounce the policy of warfare.[97] It may be mentioned that most of the inscriptions are related to the contemporary events but sometimes they touch upon the old documents either in his patron's archives or elsewhere. For example the author of the Junagadh inscription of 150 A.D., while recounting the early history of the Sudarashana Lake, says that it was created by Rashtriya Pusyagupta during the reign of Chandragupta Maurya [*c.*322-298 B.C.]. And that Yavanraja Tusaspa endowed it with irrigation canals on behalf of Asoka Maurya [c.272-232 B.C.]. "It appears that the author could see some genuine records about the lake, belonging to the 4th and 3rd centuries B.C. for the pur-pose."[98] The inscriptions give information about perso-nages and events of Indian history about which nothing is known from any other source. Only in some cases, we have recorded traditions about such subjects, the details of which can be compared with epigraphic information and we find the inscriptional evidence clothing them with interesting details.[99] We get a detailed information about the victorious campaigns of Samudragupta in Aryavarta and Dakshina-patha as well as his relations with the contemporary powers from the Allahabad Inscription of Samudragupta. However, in case of such *Prasasthis* we need to be little careful in sifting the information as there may be some degree of exaggeration in the praise of patron or some hyperbole in describing the events of his reign. There is a simple request from Meghavarna, king of Ceylon to king Samudragupta to build a monastery at Bodhgaya by sending rich presents in the form of jewels could be construed by Harisena as an "application for charter conforming him in the enjoyment of his territories"[100] The Aihole inscription of 634 A.D. gives a fair account of the rise and early history of *Chalukyas* of Badami covering a period of about one century.[101] "It has to be noticed that the treatment of the subject in the inscriptions is not as elaborate as in the works like the *Rajatarangini*. This is mainly because their space was considerably limited."[102] Another drawback with the inscriptions is that they deal with historical events and personages, but history is often shadowed in them by poetical, eulogistic and conventional elements, leaving many things to be surmised and inferred.[103] Sometimes the inscriptional evidence is incomplete, viz. the Meharauli Inscription of King Chandra. Scholars gave different opinions identifying him with Chandragupta II.[104]

Use of Eras : Dating of Inscriptions

D.C. Sircar is weary about the dating of the inscriptions; even the royal records being dated in the regnal reckoning of the rulers of the land.[105] Even in the epigraphs of the Imperial Guptas, in the earlier records, it is treated as the regnal reckoning of the particular kings, without giving it any specific name.[106] For the first time, we find the Mathura Inscription of Chandragupta II is dated both in his 5th regnal year and in the Kalanuvartamana year 61, i.e. the year 61 counted according to the (Gupta) era; other records of the Imperial Guptas mention particular years of the era either without any specification or as belonging to a particular monarch or to his reign.[107] It was of course later specifically attributed to the Guptas.[108] "It is yet unknown which early member of the Imperial Gupta dynasty founded the era, i.e. the regnal reckoning of which amongst them was continued by his successors?"[109] Since Chandragupta I, father of Samudragupta and grandfather of Chandragupta II, was the first Imperial ruler of the family, the first year of the era is generally believed by scholars to be equivalent to the year of that king's succession. This is quite probable in view of the fact that his grandson ascended the throne in the year 57 of the era, but is by no means certain. It is not at all impossible that the era started from the first regnal year of the Gupta, Ghatotkacha or Samudragupta who were respectively the grandfather, father and son of Chandragupta I. "If the spurious Nalanda and Gaya Inscriptions of respectively the 5th and 9th regnal years of Samudragupta are believed to be forged copies of two genuine records of that king bearing the said dates, the era may have started from Samudragupta's accession. But the records appear to have been copied from those of his successors".[110] If we believe that the Gupta era started with the accession of Samudragupta, then it would give a very long reign to him, i.e., A.D. 320-375. As per our analysis on the basis of inscription, Chandragupta II acted as a Dutaka (Executor) of the Nalanda grant of Samudragupta in 352-353 A.D.[111] We cannot ignore the fact that Chandragupta II married his daughter Prabhavatigupta to Vakataka crown-prince Rudra-Sena; in the event of his deceased husband after a few years she acted as the Regent Queen for her two minor sons. By collating the data on the basis of coins, inscriptions, *Puranas* and by comparing it with the chronology of the contemporary *Vakataka* and *Naga* dynasties and picking the thread from the Mathura record of Chandragupta II, year 61 of the Gupta era, i.e. A.D. 380 which being the 5th regnal year of Chandragupta II, i.e. he ascended the throne in A.D. 376.[112] The whole evidence clinches the issue in favour of Chandragupta II who seems to be the founder of the Era as earlier to Chandragupta II, no ruler has ever made mention of the Gupta era in his records though in courtesy he seems to have started it with the accession of the first imperial ruler, his grandfather *Maharajadhiraja* Chandragupta I.[113] It tallies with the first opinion expressed by D.C. Sircar who seems to have withdrawn his second option of starting it with any other ruler.[114] Similarly the inscriptional evidence certifying Ramgupta as a Maharajadhiraja and not simply a local ruler of Malwa on the basis of copper coinage, clinched the issue of his historicity as a shadowy figure of the Imperial Gupta family.[115]

Banabhatta's Harsha-Charita

A number of historical biographies of royalty were written in the period from A.D. 600 to 1200, namely the *Harsha-charita* of Banabhatta, the *Vikramankadevacharita* of Bilhana, the *Kumarapala-charitas* and the *Prithivi-raja-Vijaya* attributed to

Jayanaka. Bana's *Harshacharita* is the first work of its kind now extent, at once a biography of his great patron, Emperor Harshavardhana, and an autobio- graphy of the author. It is not only the first attempt in Indian literature at historiography but also authentic as far it goes.[116] As he was a contemporary of the Emperor, his work has very great importance as a biography. Unfortu-nately, it ends practically at the beginning of Harsha's reign and but for the description left by Hiuen Tsang, the Chinese pilgrim, we should know very little about the rest of Harsha's career. A.K. Majumdar states: "It is, therefore, clear that Bana did not want to write a history as we understand the term today, but selected an episode of Harsha's life as a literary expedient."[117] Krishnamoorthy praises Bana for giving his life sketch against the usual practice of Sanskrit poets to maintain complete silence about themselves and the times and blames his premature death[118] for leaving the 'life of Harsha' incomplete inas- much as it leaves not many of the glorious achievements in the annals of the king's eventful career and stops with the recovery of Rajyashri and Harsha's rulership of Kanouj besides Staneshvar, which, in fact, is but the beginning of his glorious reign as Emperor of India.[119] The descriptions of court and the army etc. provide us with a contemporary view of the life in the period. Bana's characterization of the leading figures in the narrative shows his deep under-standing of human nature and his insight into character and nature. It gives an intimate and reliable picture of the people, their occupations, denominations, their habits and customs, their dresses and ornaments, their beliefs, ideals and superstitions, their emotions and amusements. Thus it is of fundamental interest to the student of social history so much so that we get a full and graphic picture of the contemporary society. We get vivid accounts of life in the army camp, life in the hermitages, courtly life in the city and the calm and sequestered life of the village on the riverbank.[120] It is of interest that Bana was a Bhargava and may therefore have been inclined towards history by family tradition.[121]

Bilhana's Vikramankadevacharita

The Kashmiri poet Bilhana wrote it in about A.D. 1085. It begins with a somewhat sketchy account of Vikramaditya's father,

Someswara I (1043-1068), and then begins the life of the hero, that is Vikramaditya VI, of the Chalukya dynasty of Kaliyani (*c.*1076-1126) and ends poetically after an account of the first two years of his reign. The later part of Vikramditya's career is given in the last canto, but it is very sketchy. In between long accounts of season and court amusements, of the *Svayamvara-sabha*, of the Silahara princess, Chandralekha, the description of Vikramaditya's amusements with his wife etc., cover three cantos. The poet found it necessary to make Lord Siva appear twice and that he invented this as an excuse to cover the nefarious deed of his patron, namely insurrection against his elder brother, the rightful king and the usurpation of the throne. On the whole, the *Vikramankadevacharita* is not without historical interest, its value as history is little. Secondly, how far the exaggerated accounts of the *Svayamvara* and the nodes of royal amusement can be taken, as a true social picture of the period is doubtful. Bilhana was merely repeating the traditional way of life of an Indian king handed down from the days of Kalidasa.[122]

Padmagupta's Navasahasankacharita

Padmagupta at the beginning of the 11th century wrote an epic on the Paramara king Sindhuraja of Avanti (Malava). Though based on real events, the story of this epic is transferred into a romantic legend, in which king is united with a dragon (*naga*) princess Sasiprabha, thereby, becom-ing a universal emperor. Sindhuraja is also called the New Sahasanka (Sahasanka, was another name of Vikramaditya and will replace Vikramaditya and other great rulers of the past. The epic is entitled *Navasahasankacharita* after this name of its hero.[123]

Jayanaka's Prithvirajavijaya

The poem was written during the lifetime of Prithviraja, the unfortunate Chahamana emperor (*c.* 1177-1192), for the author himself states that he was honoured and induced to write the poem by king Prithviraja, son of Someswara. Most probably the work was composed after 1191 but before 1192 and was intended to celebrate the victory of Prithviraja over Muizz-ud-din Muhammad at the first battle of Tarain (1190-1191). Jonaraja, the author of the second *Rajatarangini* between 1450 and 1475, wrote the commentary of the poem. It is a sober historical work and the commentary is extremely useful. It is one of the most reliable sources for the history of the Chahamanas of Sakambhari.[124]

Nayachandra Suri's Hammira Mahakavya

It has been written long after the *Prithvirajavijaya.* It deals with a branch of the Chahamana dynasty, which flourished, at Ranthambhor in 1193-1301. The work derives its name from the last prince of this branch, the gallant Hammira (1282-1301). Its comparison with the contemporary Muslim chronicles proves its general accuracy, though to extol the virtues of his hero, the poet seems to have invented a *digvijaya.*[125]

Sandhyakaranandi's Ramacharita

The *Ramacharita* gives an historical account of the successful revolution in North Bengal, which cost the Pala king, Mahipala, his life and throne and of the restoration of the paternal kingdom by Ramapala, his younger brother. This great revolution, and especially the restoration, formed the main theme of the work. The technique of the composition is equally unique. Each verse of the poem has two meanings, one applicable to the story of the *Ramayana* and other to the history of the Pala kings. He calls his poem a *Ramayana* of the Kali age and describes himself as the Kalikala Valmiki.[126]

Rajataranginis

There are four *Rajataranginis*, the earliest one written by Kalhana being the most famous. Kalhana states that he began his work in the Saka year 1070 (A.D. 1148) and finished in the following year.

The *Rajatarangini* of Kalhana can be divided into three main sections. The first dealing with the mystical past, borrows heavily from the *Itihasa-Purana* tradition. In the second section, he begins to gather information from a variety of sources and there is a great degree of verifiable material. The last section deals with the history of Kashmir from the eighth to twelfth centuries and is by far the most accurate and interesting. It is largely on the basis of this section that Kalhana's significance as a critical historian can be established. Here his concern is not merely in chronicling events but also in seeking for causal explanations ranging over a wide variety of factors.[127] Kalhana had set out lofty ideal about the strict impartiality to be observed by the historians. He declares at the beginning of his work, "That virtuous poet alone is worthy of praise, who, free from love and hatred, ever restricts his language to the exposition of facts."[128] His method of writing history is almost modern: "I have examined eleven works of former scholars which contain the chronicles of kings as well as the views of sage Nila *(Nila Purana)*. By the inspection of ordinances of four kings relating to religious foundations and grants, laudatory inscriptions, as well as written records, all wearisome error has been set at rest" (I.VV. 14-15)[129]. But Kalhana did not follow his predecessors blindly. He has recorded his doubts about the lack of care in the work of Ksemendra known as the *Last of Kings*.[130] Kalhana warns the kings against interference with temple property or the rights enjoyed by the Brahmanas: "The prosperity of the kings when destroyed by the forces of kinsmen and other rivals one has been restored once more; it has no chance of being re-established if lost through disregard of the Brahmanas."

The history of Kashmir shows that Kalhana's proud assertion to the extent was justified. This can be attributed to the superior intelligence of the Brahmanas, their hold over the credulous villagers, and above all their famed capacity to carry on intrigues.[131] About women Kalhana's view is rather harsh: "Since in women's hearts there is no room for good conduct, the creator in his mercy hath guarded him with their rounded breasts." Again while describing the fidelity of a courtesan for her lover, Kalhana prefaces his grudging praise with the following observation: "Thus there are high and low courses of conduct as a result of love: taking this into consideration women have never been held deserving of either censure or adoration by those whose minds are refined" (VII, VV. 856-857). It may be said: "Kalhana was disgusted by the immoralities of certain queens, but some kings were equally immoral, and though he censures them individually, it is against women as a class that his criticism is directed."[132] Kalhana narrates the career of the kings of Kashmir in chronological order, with as much detail as is possible on obtaining from his examination of earlier works and records. Where no details are available, he merely mentions the name of the king. His delay of the contemporary is packed with full details. "It ceases to be a merely a chronicle of dry details and faithfully presents the ebb and flow of national life, the period of glory and misery, and the greatness and weakness of men and rulers, in short, all those minute details which make history a record of intense human interest, faithfully portraying the march of events through which a people works out its own destiny."[133]

Kalhana's historical writing, although it owes a great deal to the *Itihasa* and *Purana* tradition, is nevertheless a departure from it. There is a noticeable change in the character of causal relationships between the first and last sections, where supernatural elements give way to rational, secular explanations, sometimes based on empirical observation. The fact that Kalhana and his family were intimately associated with the politics of Kashmir during the eleventh and twelfth centuries may impart account for this change. The *Rajatarangini* is often regarded as somehow outside the Indian tradition because of its highly developed historical sense. Some scholars attribute this to the influence of the Greeks – a thousand years prior to the writing of the book – or the influence of the Turks in Central Asia who, because they were converted to Islam, are immediately endowed with a historiographical tradition. Romila Thapar considers it a part of Indian tradition with some influence of the Buddhist tradition on Kalhana.[134]

Historical biographies in Sanskrit declined after the conquest of many parts of Northern India by the Turks and Afghans. Now the majority of the court-poets were Muslims who wrote in Persian. However, Kashmir remained an exception in this case. "The *Rajataranginis* are the only works in Sanskrit which deal with the history of Muslim monarchs, and the fact that the

Sultans, instead of employing Persian scholars, employing these Pandits to write their Chronicles proves the high esteem in which they were held."[135] The *Rajataranginis* were translated into Persian more than once, and the famous Muslim historians, such as Nizam-ud-din, Farishta, and Abul Fazl, unhesitatingly followed them as their only source for the history of Kashmir.[136]

Dvitiya Rajatarangini

By Jonaraja who lived during the reign of great Sultan Zain-ul-Abiden (*c.*1411-1463) who is justly regarded as Akbar of Kashmir. Jonaraja personally had an occasion to complain to the king about the forgery made by the purchaser in his inherited property, instead of purchase of one plot, they clearly wrote ten and appropriated the entire property of ten plots *(prastha)* of his father Nonaraja inherited from Laularaja. The king immersed the document in water, so that the forged letters were washed off and the original came out. Thus says the grateful historian: "The King's fame increased, the guilty were punished and I received my land".[137]

Actually Sri Siryabhatta was employed by king Zain-ul-Abiden to write a history of former kings from Jayasimha of Kashmir who asked Jonaraja to write the history. Jonaraja who modestly adds has disclosed this: "I have written an epitome of the history of the kings; may some clever poet write it properly."[138]

Tritiya Rajatarangini

After Jonaraja's death in the year 35 (Kaliyuga year 4535; A.D. 1435) Pandit Srivara took the mantle of his guru Jonaraja. Srivara starts his history from the middle of Zain-ul-Abiden's reign; that is, he continues his narrative from where his guru Jonaraja's ended. Srivara was as modest as his predecessor. His readers are invited to go through his work to learn the activities of the kings and not to enjoy Kavya and he laments the fact that he has compiled records like the Kayasthas, from which other scholars in the future would be able to produce a *lalita-kavya.*[139]

Chaturtha Rajatarangini

The fourth *Rajatarangini* is the work of two authors, Prajyabhatta and Suka. Prajyabhatta wrote a work called *Rajavalipataka*, which recorded the accounts up to the year 89 (Kaliyuga year 4589; A.D 1489). Since no other poet took up the work any further, Suka took upon himself to give an account of kings. Suka does not give his data and his history ends with the arrival of Asaf Khan to Kashmir. The concluding position, however, deals with the arrival of Akbar and the subsequent history of Kashmir, which seems to be later interpolation.[140] The *Rajataranginis* are the only works in Sanskrit, which deal with the history of Muslim monarchs.

Gujarat Chronicles

Gujarat tradition of writing historical chronicles is unique in India. Large number of chronicles were written about the Chalukyas of Gujarat (940-1305). None of them, however, can be termed 'history', but they provide rough materials for writing one. A.K. Majumdar gives a long list of 17 *Kavyas* in this respect. Some of the information is of great value not to be found anywhere else.[141]

It may be remarked that the *Itihasa-Purana* was kept alive when the court-poets associated their subject of the biography with the earlier heroes and legends. This seems to be largely an attempt at literary ornamentation and at continuing the *Itihasa* tradition.

"Unfortunately, modern historians have tended to discuss the historicity of the biographies largely because of the literary ornamentation."[142] The authors of these texts were generally Brahmanas who maintained the close affinity between the *Purana* and the historical biography. The only difference being that these works focused attention on a particular person or on a single dynasty and concentrated on a small time-span as well as a precisely defined geographical area. The historical frame was now much smaller and allowed a greater detail.[143]

Buddhist Historiography

It provides us with the Buddhist version of the early evolution of society and civilization. "The *Tripitaka* is in principle a record of important episodes in the life of the Buddha, including the discourses in which he formulated his doctrines *(Sutrapitaka)* and the events connected with the foundation of his 'community' *(Sangha)* and the enactment of its rulers of organization and discipline (*Vinayapitaka*). It provides us with a great deal of information about India in the time of the Buddha (566-486 B.C.), especially on account of the circumstantial nature of the record.[144] We know about society and cultural life as well as about economics and political events. The *Digha Nikaya* of the *Sutrapitaka* includes the discourses, mostly attributed to the Buddha, which include the ancient history and some other accounts of ancient events. The *Vinayapitaka* in describing the foundation of the Buddhist community and proceeding apparently in chronological order to record the subsequent events in that 'community', in fact began a history of Buddhism. The record was continued after the *Parinirvana* of the Buddha, to include certain events of a century later in the community (during the reign of Asoka, the Black of Magadha), in the *Vinayapitaka* itself. Sometime after that (most probably 349 B.C.), the Buddhist community split and separate schools continued to keep their historical records separately, not including them in the *Tripitaka*. It makes the beginning of the traditions of interpretation, a history called *Vamsa* in Ceylon (Now Sri Lanka),[145] connecting the record of the activities of the Buddha, more or less a direct record of events – the Buddhist chronicles of Ceylon, connected with Indian Tradition, namely the *Dipavamsa* and the *Mahavamsa*. These chronicles began as an oral tradition and were recorded in writing at a later period, their present form dating to about the 5th and 6th centuries A.D. Out of the two texts, the *Dipavamsa* is more narrow in its interests as it narrates the history of the island. The *Mahavamsa* is connected with the Mahavihara monastery in Ceylon and the authorship is attributed to a monk called Mahanama. The destruction of the Mahavihara monastery in the fourth century A.D. disrupted the records. It has been suggested that the material was then collated from various monastic sources. "The purpose in writing the chronicles was partly historical and partly didatic since they were also intended for the edification of the Buddhist Order, *Sangha*."[146]

Jain Historiography

Apart from the *Pauranik* and the Buddhist tradition we have a third tradition, i.e. Jain Historiography. The Jina being a contemporary of the Buddha, the Jain histories cover the same period as the Buddha. The Jainas too had their conception of cycles of social evolution and their own version of the more ancient history of the celebrated emperors. Their earlier texts have been less well preserved than those of the Buddhists, so that their present 'canon' (of the Swetambara school, no other version survives) is late recension containing some texts perhaps as much as a thousand years later than Jina. Among the earliest texts in this canon *Acaranga* (end of the 4th century B.C.) records some episodes in the life of the Jina. The *Vyakhyaprajnapti* (perhaps 1st century A.D.) amplifies these and we see the same shift from history into legend, which we find in the Buddhist tradition. It gives the ancient cyclic history while the legend of the Jina culminates in the *Jinacharita* (part of the *Kalpasutra*). The *Stananga* a little earlier (1st century B.C.) also gives this, with the twelve universal emperors of the present cycle in India (Bharata, the Southern Continent, there are supposed to be others in the Northern Continent), its 24 *Jinas*, 9 *Baladevàs* (including Rama, the Solar king of Puranic tradition), 9 *Vasudevas* (including Krsna), their enemies (*Pratisatrus*, Ravana and others) and the legislators of mankind (Manus as in the *Puranas*), other canonical sources for this universal and apparently almost entirely mythical history are *Smavayanga* (a kid of supplement to the *Sthananga*), *Antakrtadaska*, *Jnatadharmakatha* and *Jambudvipaprajnapti*. The *Jnatadharmakatha* includes the Jain version of the *Mahabharata*. Another version of the *Mahabharata* is the *Harivamsa-purana* of Jinasena (A.D. 783), the best-known version being the *Parisista-parvan* of Hemachandra (12th century), which includes the kings of Magadha down to the Mauryas.[147]

The Jainas typically debunked the Brahmanical history and myth by making the stories more rational, eliminating supernatural interventions. They have objected to Rama's depiction as a demon and monster while he was a Wizard (*Vidyadhara*) though they accepted his folly in abduction of

Rama's wife.[148] Jinasena (9th century) wrote an *Adipurana,* a complete universal history, which comprises a history of 63 famous men (emperors, Jinas, etc.) of the present cycle, which was completed (*Uttarapurana*) by Gunabhadra. Jinasena (II) has some interesting discussions on the idea and scope of history, the original ideal society and the development of civilization etc.[149] The canonical *Nandi* and *Avasyakasutra* give a list of Jain teachers during the centuries following the Jina, this inaugurating the history of Jainism and of the period of Indian history after the Jina. There are many lists (*Pattavalis* and *Guruvavalis*) and legends of teachers in Jain schools, which contribute to general Indian chronology. The Jainas continued[150] the historical tradition in writing of the *Prabandhas*, connected narratives relating to royalty and used them to moralize on the actions of reigning kings.[151] The other literature consisted of genealogies and chronicles pertaining to local kings and states. Merutunga's *Prabandhachintamani*, Jinaprabha's *Vividha-tirthakalpa* and Rajasekhara's (14th century) *Prabandhakosi*. The legend of Vikramaditya is also covered in part in the anonymous *Kalkacharyaka-thanaka*. Yativrsabha's *Tiloyapannatti* on cosmology also contains information on history (Guptas : I : 95-9). The survival of such histories or biographies is seen generally to depend on their literary rather than their historical merit.[152]

Chief Features of Indian Historical Tradition

There are three major characteristic forms – genealogies, myths and historical narrative and these three are frequently interwoven in the texts. The core of the historical tradition was the genealogical records. These genealogical sections in the *Puranas* are embedded in a larger whole made up of myths, cosmological theories and social and ritualistic laws, which provides a room to dismiss the entire text as fanciful.[153] Genealogies are also useful as records of time. The span of time can be calculated through the generations in the genealogies. Similarly a record of regnal years can indicate the time span of a dynasty. It is not surprising that in the genealogies of both the *Puranas* and the Pali chronicles, the more recent genealogies are the more accurate. Secondly, the inclusion of myths is relevant to the historical world-view of the authors of these texts. The great flood caused the total destruction of the world and this is a recognized stage in the cyclic time concept. The beginnings of history therefore emerge from the very beginning. The word Manu provided the generic base for *manava* meaning 'mankind'.[154]

The third characteristic, historical narrative often contains the core of historical explanation. It examines the ideological assumptions implicit in the historical narrative. The two most important assumptions are, firstly, the notion of time, and secondly, the role of man in shaping history, and the two are interrelated.[155] The measurement of time changes and evolves in keeping with historical changes in a society. In historical terms, the use of a calendar also suggests the use of eras. In India, the earliest evidence of the use of an era dates to the first century B.C., the previous reckoning having been in regnal years. We know of the Krta or Vikrama era of 58 B.C. and the Saka of A.D. 78. From the Gupta period onwards there is a flowering of eras all over the subcontinent. The reference to the *Mahabharata* war to *Circa* 3102 B.C. by the Hindus and the Buddha's death have been attempted to be used as an era date. The Hindu tradition as recorded in the *Puranas* saw a time as moving in a cycle – the *Mahayuga* – the great cycle, which lasts for 4,320,000 years. The cycle was divided into four parts – *Krta*, *Treta*, *Dvapara* and *Kaliyuga*. The *Kaliyuga*, is the current period of time which we are living, which started in about 3102 B.C. The theory of *Mahayuga*, cyclic time also subsumed the idea of changing morals. The beginning of the cycle is a period of pristine bliss and an abundance of virtue. But gradually virtue gives way to evil until finally the *Kaliyuga*, the last of the four parts of the cycle, becomes an evil age *per se*. Evil is uprooted in the final destruction and the new cycle starts afresh with a period of virtue. The Hindu cyclical concept was, in fact, a cosmological concept. It did not deter the recording of the past in a form considered socially relevant and necessary to the present and the future. The Buddhists believed time to be of incalculable length and pre-supposed a movement of time in waves, beginning with a golden age gradually degenerating into evil, which is finally overcome by a slow return to a utopian state.[156]

The historical explanation was interwoven with the two concepts of *Dharma* and *Karma*. *Dharma* was seen as in the historical context, as the socio-religious ordering of society and events were illustrations of the religious, moral and social maxims, which shaped the *Dharma* system. This introduced to some degree elements of historical determinism as well as the idea of the responsibility of the individual in history[157] as earlier explained by us in the tradition of boon and curse, which are related to causation even relegating to the background of previous births. Normally, theory of historical inevitability would tend to overrule the search for varied historical explanation, which in Indian context was covered by multiple episodes connected with the same event of the previous or earlier births, mythological or real. The concept of *Karma* concerns the actions in the life of an individual, which condition his next birth. It is closely associated with the idea of *punya* or merit, which helps an explanation for the facts and events of the present birth. "From the perspective of historical explanation, the concept of *karma* frequently provides the channel for historical explanation."[158] This attributed to an extreme idea of fate or destiny over, which man has no control which, only can be modified by the intervention of the supernatural. "Men die and on occasion are restored to life by the will of gods. Famines, pestilences and times of trouble can also be attributed to the will of the gods. Divine retribution against evil actions or divine intervention in battle are not unknown."[159] This brought a third dimension in Indian tradition, the theory of incarnation and the doctrine of *Bhakti* to seek divine intervention in the time of distress as enunciated in the *Srimad Bahgvad Gita*.[160]

The core of Indian historical tradition consists of the *Itihasa-Purana* tradition, which is stated to have been refurbished in the post-Gupta period, though it remained scattered and undocumented in the pre-Gupta period. Though the *Puranas* formed a genre of scared literature, it is not a static tradition, for it has changed its form over the centuries. Historical changes of various kinds in the post-Gupta period brought out the historical writing, which, was always regarded as secular.

In India the political power was not given so much importance, as was the lineage and chronicle of the group: hence the importance given to genealogies "continuity was seen not in the sequence of political events but more often in the sequence of the lineage. Political history was not therefore the pivot of Indian historical tradition as it was in the Greek historical tradition."[161] It did, however, gradually become important in the historical literature of the post-Gupta period. Historical biographies, family chronicles and regional histories, later in date, are the more secular extension of this tradition and form the main corpus of historical writing.[162]

Father of History

We may state that our scholarship has been usually Euro-centric. Whatever the European scholars say in the matter even without any rhyme or reason we admit in the academia as a gospel truth till the hammer of a solid truth uproots it; still it is not swallowed easily as some west-oriented scholars always echo the falsehood. The dating of the Vedas by Max-Muller or the theory of Aryan invasion on India are the best examples.

Another example is that earlier Herodotus, the Greek historian was given the status of 'Father of history', which has now been shifted to German scholar Ranke in the 19th century.

The latest explanation of history is history of Culture or Cultural history. The dynasties and the kings die out but the Culture remains and survives even in an integrated form if not in the 'pure' form considering Culture as an epitome of history, we have to reconsider the whole matter and assign the high status of 'Father of History' to Krsna Dvaipayna Veda Vyasa who fits in the criteria and also predates Herodotus as well as Ranke.

Veda Vyasa has played a great historical role in compiling the *Vedas,* the *Puranas* and is the author of the *Mahabharata* on the invocation of Lord Brahma while Lord Ganesh himself acted as a scribe to preserve all the traditional lore. The *Mahabharata* has been hailed as the fifth Veda. Krsna Dvaipayan has been named as 28th Vyasa in Indian tradition,[163] which is upheld by Alberuni (A.D. 1030).[164]

The *Mahabharata* calls itself as *Itihasa-Purana*, *Kavya* and *Akhyana* in the introductory portion. It is called *Mahabharata* because in it is narrated the great life history of the Bharatas. The epic itself explains the name – "The work is called *Mahabharata* on account of its greatness, enormity in size and weightness, suggesting that it overweighs the Veda and other sacred literature in India."[165] The Bharatas, forming the subject of the *Mahabharata* are mentioned as the warrior-tribe in the *Rgveda* with their habitat between the Ganga and the Yamuna. The old heroic poem, dealing with the bloody family feud resulting in the overthrow of the Kauravas by the Pandavas, forms the nucleus of the *Mahabharata*.

The nucleus assumed the present form of the *Mahabharata* by periodical additions of matter of different kinds including:

(i) Legendary matter from the bardic lore,
(ii) Myths and legends of Brahmanical origin,
(iii) Cosmological, genealogical and geographical matter in the nature of *Puranas* and local myths,
(iv) Myths of Visnu, and, later of Siva,
(v) Fables, parables, fairy tales and moral stories,
(vi) Ascetic poetry, and
(vii) Prose pieces and Brahmanical legends and moral tales, entirely or partly in prose.

The inclusion of this diverse matter, which has made the *Mahabharata* at once a Kavya, Sastra, Sruti, Law, Philosophy etc. indicates the uniform popularity of the Great Epic through the ages and the anxiety of the compilers to make the *Mahabharata* an encyclopaedia for all time. The statement in the epic that whatever is (incorporated) here may be found elsewhere; but what is not found here cannot be got anywhere else. Originally Vyasa composed a *Bharata* of 24,000 verses and *Mahabharata* to be of 1,00,000 verses. Macdonell and others take the extent of Vyasa's work to be of 8,800.[166] The big epic the *Mahabharata* has seen three recessions, namely *'Jaya'*, *'Bharata'* and finally, the *Mahabharata* is also certified by information based on tradition.[167] The epic itself speaks of its three different beginnings:

(i) *Manvadi,* i.e. from the very beginning of the extent *Mahabharata*, after the *mangala-sloka 'Narayanam namaskrtya',* etc. according to the critical edition, followed by the conversation between Sauti (or Suta etc.) and the sages at Saunaka's hermitage;

(ii) *Astikadi,* i.e. from the description of the Janmejaya's *Sarpasatra*, where begins the *Astikaparvan,* and

(iii) *Uparicaradi,* i.e. from the commencement of the actual narration of the history of the Bharatas, where begins the *Amsavataraparvan.*[168]

These are the different beginnings of the *Mahabharata* as recited respectively by Suta, Vaisampayana and Vyasa. Thus Suta's narration begins from the first *adhyaya* itself, that of Vaisampayana from the *adhyaya* 13, and that of Vyasa from *adhyaya* 54 of the critical edition. These three are said to be the beginnings respectively of *Mahabharata*, *Bharata* and *Jaya* and the extent of the *Bharata* and the *Mahabharata* is said to be 24,000 and 1,00,000. There is also a view that the original *Bharata* comprising 24,000 *slokas* has been expanded to one of 1,00,000 *slokas* by the addition of episodes, etc. It has been explained: "The meaning of the *Bharata*, in so far as it is a relation of facts and events of which Sri Krsna and the Pandavas are connected, is called *Astikadi* (historical). That interpretation by which, we find lessons on *Dharma, Bhakti* and other gods is called *Manvadi* (religious and moral). Thirdly, the interpretation by which every sentence, word or syllable is shown to be the declaration of the Almighty Ruler of the Universe is called *Auparicara* (Transcendental)."[169] The Epic is supposed to be developed between 400 B.C. to A.D. 400 though according to Pusalker, the Bharata war was fought in c.1400 B.C.[170]

The critical edition has 16 Sub-*Parvans* and 299 *adhyayas,* it presents the shortest text compared with the Culcutta, Bombay and Madras editions.[171] It may be mentioned that the episodic material, comprising of ancient *gathas*, *anuvamsa,* stanzas, stories, descriptions, discussions, discourses on moral, ethical and philosophical topics etc., in the *Mahabharata* is not a subsequent elaboration secondarily introduced but formed part of the original epic, its purpose in the epic being to fill up the "temporal hiatuses" in the narrative (viz. twelve years' exile etc.). There close and striking semblances between many of these stories as found in the *Mahabharata* and the *Puranas*. "Though in a few cases, the assumption of independent common source may be correct, in most cases compilers of the late versions of the *Puranas* have drawn their material from the *Mahabharata* Narratives."[172] The critical edition, besides giving the critical text, gives a digest of the manuscript tradition of the *Mahabharata* extending over nearly a thousand years.[173] About the chronology of the *Bharata* war, it is well known that the orthodox view holds the *Bharata* war to have taken place about 5000 years ago. Dr. Triveda, on the basis of historical works, astronomy etc., concluded that the war was fought in 3137 B.C. while other scholars ascribe to different dates.[174] According to Aryabhata tradition the date is stated to be 3102, which is the tradition, carried down to us.[175]

It was Vyasa himself who gave the story of *Mahabharata* to mankind. It is many years after the *Mahabharata* war, exhorted by Lord Brahma thus: "You have witnessed the *Mahabharata* war, you knew intimately all the heroes who lived in those days. You knew of everything that happened. It will be an excellent thing if you write the story of the *Mahabharata*."[176]

While Vyasa was contemplating as to the best means of transmitting the poem to his disciples, Brahma appeared and in response to Vyasa's prayer suggested Ganesa as the scribe. Ganesa agreed on condition that his pen did not cease writing for a moment. He further agreed to Vyasa's request to cease to continue writing whenever he failed to comprehend anything. By way of diversion Vyasa knit in the epic a number of Kutaslokas (riddles) to puzzle the divine scribe. The number of such *slokas* is said to be 8800.[177]

"Vyasa laid the foundations of *Itihasa* and *Purana* – history and tradition. He is perhaps the first historian of the human race."[178] The vision of Vyasa gradually encom-passed life in one vast concept of *Dharma* in all its bearings, in the strength and weakness of man; in the nature of human relationship, in the imponderable forces working in the universe, in the universal moral order supported by *Satya*, *Tapas*, and *Shanti*, truth, self-discipline and the all embracing realm of the spirit.[179]

The scene of the Epic is the ancient kingdom of the Kurus which flourished along the upper course of the Ganges; and the historical fact on which the Epic is based is a great war which, took place between the Kurus and a neighbouring tribe, the Panchalas, in the thirteenth or fourteenth century before Christ.[180]

According to the Epic, Pandu and Dhritarashtra, who was born blind, were brothers. Pandu died early, and Dhritarashtra, became king of the Kurus, and brought up the five sons of Pandu along with his hundred sons... Yudhisthira was the son of Dharma or virtue, Bhima of Vayu or Wind, Arjuna of Indra or Rain god, the twin youngest were the sons of Aswin twins, and Karna was the son of Surya, the Sun, but was believed by himself and by all others to be the son of a simple chariot-driver.[181]

Duryodhana was the eldest son of Dhritarashtra and was jealous of his cousins, the sons of Pandu, Yudhisthira, the eldest son of Pandu, was a man of truth and piety.

The education of the princes being finished, Dhrita-rashtra put Yudhisthira, the eldest son of Pandu, on the throne of his father. The sterling virtue of Yudhisthira and the valour and devotion of his other brothers aroused jealousies in the hearts of the sons of the blind king. At the instigation of Duryodhana, the eldest of them, the five Pandava brothers were prevailed upon to visit Varnavat, on the plea of a religious festival that was being held there. They were accommodated in the palace made under Duryodhana's instructions of hemp, resin and lac and other inflammable materials, which were subsequently set to fire secretly. But the good Vidura, the step-brother of Dhrita-rashtra, having become cognizant of the evil intentions of Duryodhana and his party, had warned the Pandavas of the plot, and they managed to escape without anyone's knowledge. When the Kurus saw the house was reduced to ashes, they heaved a sigh of relief and thought all obstacles were now removed out of their path. Then the children of Dhritarashtra got hold of the kingdom.

The five Pandava brothers had fled to the forest with their mother Kunti and lived in exile. In the meanwhile with feat of bravery in a *Svayamvara* arranged by king Drupada, famed king of the Panchalas for his daughter Draupadi, Arjuna married Draupadi who became the common wife of the five brothers as blessed by their mother by a mistake of communication and mother's words were obeyed, which seems to be evidently a glimpse of the past polyandrous stage. The objection to this marriage was settled at the intervention of Vyasa who made King Drupada yield to this polyandrous marriage, stating that such a marriage was allowed to those princes and it was permitted, and the princess was married to the five sons of Pandu.[182]

Then the Pandavas lived in peace and prosperity. Though Duryodhana and his party conceived of fresh plots to destroy them. King Dhritarashtra was prevailed upon by the wise counsels of the elders to make peace with the Pandavas and so he invited them home amidst the rejoicings of the people and gave them half of the kingdom. Then, the five brothers built for themselves a beautiful city, called Indraprastha, and extended their dominions laying all the people under tribute to them. Then, the eldest brother Yudhisthira even successfully performed a Rajasuya sacrifice. Even the Kauravas were invited to come and take a share of the performance of sacrifice. At the conclusion of the sacrifice, Yudhisthira was crowned emperor, and declared as lord paramount. Duryodhana, out of jealousy devised plans to affect their fall as he knew to overcome them by force was beyond his power.

Yudhisthira had the love of gambling and he was challenged at an evil hour to play dice with Shakuni, the crafty gambler and the evil genius of Duryodhana. Shakuni and his party had made false dice. So Yudhisthira lost game after game, staking everything he had, and losing all, until his possessions, his kingdom and everything were lost. The last stage came when, under further challenge, he had no other resources left but to stake his brothers, and then himself, and last of all, the fair Draupadi, and lost all. Now they were completely at the mercy of the Kauravas who cast all sorts of insults on them, and subjected Draupadi to most inhuman treatment. At last through the intervention of the blind king, they got their liberty, and were asked to return home and rule their kingdom. But Duryodhana saw the danger and forced his father to allow one more throw of dice in which the party which would lose should retire to forests for twelve years, and then live unrecognized in a city for one year; but if they were found out, the same term of exile should have to be undergone once again and then only the kingdom was to be restored to the exiled. This game Yudhisthira lost also, and the five brothers retired to the forests with Draupadi, as homeless exiles. They lived in the forests and mountains for twelve years. There they performed many deeds of virtue and valour and would go out now and then on a long round of pilgrimages, visiting many holy places. "That part of the poem is very interesting and instructive, and various are the incidents, tales and legends with which this part of the book is replete. There are in it beautiful and sublime stories of ancient India, religious and philosophical. Great sages came to see the brothers in their exile, and narrated to them many telling stories of ancient India, so as to make them bear lightly the burden of their exile."[183]

Now as the thirteenth year of the exile was drawing near, a Yaksha bade them go to Virata's kingdom and live there in such disguises, as they would think best. Accordingly they served king Virata in different capacities. Thus concealing their identity the Pandava brothers safely spent a year and were discovered just when the year was out. Soon after negotiations for peaceful settlement of half of the kingdom in their favour were started by Yudhisthira but Duryodhana would not consent to their legitimate demands and declared that he would not yield without fight even as much land as a needle's point would hold. Dhritarashtra pleaded again and again for peace, but all in vain. Even the efforts on behalf of Krishna and the elders of the royal court went futile. So, at last preparations were made on both sides for war, and all the warlike nations took part in it. The war lasted eighteen days. Indeed, out of the eighteen *Aksauhinis* of soldiers very few men were left. The death of Duryodhana ended the war in favour of the Pandavas. The lament of Gandhari; the queen, and the widowed women, and the funerals of the deceased warriors followed it.

"The greatest incident of the war was the marvellous and immortal poem of the *Gita*, the *Song Celestial*. It is the popular scripture of India and the loftiest of all teachings. It consists of a dialogue held by Arjuna with Krishna just before the commencement of the fight on the battlefield of Kurukshetra."[184]

After the conclusion of the Kurukshetra war, the great warrior and venerable grandsire, Bhishma, who fought ten days out of the eighteen days' battle, still lay on his death-bed, and gave instructions to Yudhisthira on various subjects, such as the duties of the king, the duties of the four castes, the four stages of life, the laws of marriage, the bestowing of gifts etc., basing them on the teachings of ancient sages, which covered the Sankhya and Yoga philosophy, narration of numerous tales and traditions about saints, gods and kings. "These teachings occupy nearly one-fourth of the entire work and form an invaluable store-house of Hindu laws and moral codes."[185] Yudhisthira, crowned as King, on the advice of Vyasa performed the Asvamedha sacrifice.

After the war, for fifteen years, Dhritarashtra dwelt in peace and honour, obeyed by Yudhisthira and his brothers. Then the aged monarch leaving Yudhisthira on the throne, retired to the forest with his devoted wife and Kunti, the mother of the Pandava brothers, to pass his last days in asceticism.

Thirty-six years had now passed since Yudhisthira regained his empire. Then came to him the news that Krishna had left his mortal body. Krishna, the sage, his friend, his prophet, his counsellor, had departed. Arjuna hastened to Dwaraka and came back to confirm the sad news that Krishna and the Yadavas were all dead. Then, the king and other brothers, overcome with sorrow declared that the time for them to go, too, had arrived. So they cast off the burden of royalty, placed Parikshita, the grandson of Arjuna, on the throne, and retired to the Himalayas, on the great journey, the *Mahaprasthana*.

Thus the story of the *Mahabharata*, sets in a sublime poem the triumph of virtue and defeat of vice.

We quote one example. When Draupadi urged king Yudhisthira to attack the Kurus, after he had been so cruelly cheated and ruined by them, the wise king pointed out to her that the returning of the evil for evil could only result in the continuance of misery. "The wise man, who though persecuted, suffereth not his wrath to be aroused, joyeth in the other world, having passed his persecutor over with indifference. For this reason it has been said that a wise man whether strong or weak, should ever forgive his persecutor, even when the latter is in straits... If amongst men there were not some equal to the earth in forgiveness, there would be no peace among men, but continued strife born of wrath. If the injured were to return their injuries, if one chastised by his superior were to chastise his superior in return, the consequence would be the destruction of every creature, and sin would prevail. If the man who hath ill speeches from another returneth those speeches; if the injured man returneth his injuries; if the chastised person chastises in return, then would fathers slay sons, and sons fathers; then would husbands slay wives, and wives husbands; then, O Krsna, how could birth take place in a world thus filled with anger? For know thou that the birth of creatures is due to peace."[186] Similarly Yudhisthira, who was an epitome of *Dharma,* responded to his brother Bhima, giving way to fierce anger in the dark days of their exile bitterly upbraid his elder with "the trite merit of stocking to a promise" made to gamblers who had over-reached him, laid the loss of kingdom. But Yudhisthira, summoning all his patience and remaining silent for a few moments, answered gently that all Bhima's words were true: "I cannot reproach thee for torturing me thus, piercing me with the arrowy words, from my own folly alone has this calamity fallen upon you all. I should have controlled my mind, and not to allow it to be influenced by arrogance, vanity and pride. I cannot then reproach thee, O Bhima, for thy winged words. Yet have I given my pledge, and who may break his pledged word? Death is easier to bear than gaining of a realm by a lie. What avail then, to speak to me thus harshly? My heart is broken by the sight of the sufferings I have caused. But I may not break my word. Wait, O my brother, for the return of the better days, as the sower waits for the harvest. For know, O Bhima, that my promise may not be made untrue. Virtue is better than life itself or than the joys of heaven. Kingdom, sons, fame, wealth, all these do not come up to one-sixteenth part of truth." Thus patiently did the prince bear his brother's angry taunts, and ever was he ready to meet harsh blame with gentle humility, and to win by love a yielding that has proud brothers would never have given to wrath."[187]

The *Mahabharata* states: "He who is not angry with the angry, he is a physician unto both. He saveth himself as well as the others from great danger."[188] "Addressed harshly, let him not reply harshly. The wrath of the wrathful assailant consumeth himself, and taketh away all his merit."[189]

Thus we see that the *Mahabharata* is not only an Epic of War but also a repository of knowledge on *Dharma, Rajadharma,* society, polity and culture for a period of about one thousand years, i.e. 800 B.C. to A.D. 500. It is of an encyclopaedic nature and has been known as the fifth Veda *"Bharatam Panchamo Vedah"*.[190]

"The epic literature in India consists of *Itihasa* and *Purana,* which convey the sense of the epic and the *Pancalaksana,* the former comprising the *Mahabharata* and the *Ramayana* and the latter the *Maha-Puranas* and *Upa-Puranas*. The study of *Itihasa* and *Purana* has been rightly stressed as necessary for the correct interpretation of the Vedas.[191]

It may be stated that the epics have been written by great sages Vyasa and Valmiki, which have been known as *Itihasa* in Indian tradition, which tell the story of great royal dynasties based in time and space and not at all based on in figment of imagination. Similarly, the *Puranas* and the *Up-Puranas* depict the royal genealogies along with theory of universal creation, fasts, festivals, deities, *tirthas* (places of religious significance) as well as the portrayal of the culture in space and time; and the genre *'charitas'*, 'Biographies' are based on the contemporary royal dynasties or personages each one having its own style of narration. If the *Mahabharata* and the *Ramayana* have been authored by famous sages like Vyasa and Valmiki, the *Puranas* by the Bhrgu-Angirasas who were Brahmanas or the Sutas and Magadhas (not necessarily to be Brahmanas) who carried the tradition, or the Biographers who were generally Brahmanas and contemporary court-poets how can we believe in the lack of sense in Indian historiography as Brown seems to be bent upon denigrating Indian historiography; making all efforts in picking up passages when well-known scholars[192] have washed out the blames on Indian historiography, disagreeing with them and deliberately concluding Indian historiography as faulty and inferior in comparison to historiography in the West as well as

South Asia, in particular China which he over-praises.[193] We may mention that the criticism by Brown is guided by prejudice, bias and partiality. Each country has his own tradition and genre of writing history.

In case of India it had a very strong oral tradition, which once for all at one time brought into writing and is stated to have been refurbished during the period A.D. 400-500, i.e. the Gupta period. As the tradition goes Lord Rama belonged to the *Treta* epoch where the degeneration of morality was in lesser degree which got further worse during the *Dvapara* age when Lord Krishna appeared and finally the *Kaliyuga* started which is worst period impregnated with the collapse of all morality after leaving the earth by Lord Krishna who lived for 36 years after the *Mahabharata war* which took place in 3102 B.C. According to the tradition we may believe the beginning of Kaliyuga by 3138 B.C.[194] Truly it has been said "What is not in it is not found elsewhere" centuries have gone by; empires have risen and fallen; the outlook of man has changed in many aspects; but the *Mahabharata* stands changeless as human nature, reflecting the universal experience of man. We learn how due to harsh words spoken by Draupadi to Duryodhana created a knot for ever: "Blind man's son is blind too" saying this laughing Draupadi when Duryodhana slipped and fell in the palace of the Pandavas, mistaking the glass floor for water. "Draupadi's words of mockery set the stage for battle in the *Mahabharata*."[195]

It delineates reality of human behaviour: "the greed, jealousy, deceit and adamancy leading to strife by the Kauravas and the weakness of Yudhisthira towards gambling which brought calamity to the Pandavas time and again – the art of gambling has been condemned in the Rgveda."[196]

"The *Puranas* rightly call Vyasa the Manu of this age. He is India's real architect and guide – not of the stretch of land measured by the geographers and assessed by economists, but of the real, living and breathing India, the Bharat, which has survived through the ages and that will have to lead mankind into the light in the time to come.[197]

It should be remembered that in India we find the mention of historians or the legendaries (*Etihasikas*) in Yaska's *Nirukta* (7th-5th century B.C.). While explaining about Vrtra: Waters march against, i.e. know (the secret) outlet of Vrtra whose enemy is Indra, i.e. Indra is his slayer or destroyer, therefore, he (is called) having Indra as his enemy. But who is Vrtra? 'It is a cloud' say the etymologists (It is a demon, son of Tvasta, say the legendarians)[198] (*Etihasaka*). The phenomenon is rain is produced by the comingling of water (vapours) and lightning (*jyotis*). With reference to this there are figurative descriptions of battle. Indeed, the descriptions of Vedic stanzas and the narratives of the Brahmanas (depict him) no doubt, as a serpent. [In the folklore they say when there is a sparkling among thundering of the clouds, that god Indra is beating demon Vrtra with his thunderbolt]. By expanding his body, he blocked the channels (of the rivers). When he was killed, waters flowed forth. The following is the stanza which explains this: "Having the demon as their master, and the cloud as their guardian, the obstructed waters stood (behind) as kine (held back) by a merchant. He slew Vrtra, and reopened that outlet of water which had been closed."[199] In the *Nirukta*, the word *Itihasa* is used to cite history (or legend). King Rishtisena had two sons, namely Devapi and Santanu who belonged to the clan of the Kurus. Santanu, the younger brother, caused himself to be installed as king. Devapi retired to practise austerities. From that time the god did not rain for twelve years in the kingdom of Santanu. The Brahmanas said to him: "Thou hast committed (an act of) unrighteousness. Because thou hast caused thyself to be installed as king, having put thy elder brother aside, therefore, the god does not rain in thy kingdom." Then he, i.e. Santanu sought to invest Devapi with sovereignty. To him said Devapi: Let me be thy priest and sacrifice for thee. Here is his hymn expressing a desire for rain: "The seer Devapi son of Rstisena, acting as the performing priest (*Purohita*), knew (how to obtain) the goodwill of the gods. He caused the divine waters to flow from the upper to the lower ocean by means of rain."[200]

Thus shows that history had emerged as an Independent discipline in India by the 7th – 5th century B.C. Another lesson we learn from the *Mahabharata* from the Ganesha-Vyasa dialogue is that we should not write anything without fully understanding it.

REFERENCES

1. Philip P. Weiner (ed.) *Dictionary of the History of Ideas*, Charles Scribner's, New York, 1973, p.464.
2. The *New Encyclopaedia Britannica*, Vol 8, p.946.
3. Wiener, *op. cit.*, pp. 465-466.
4. R.G. Collingwood, *The Idea of History*, OUP, 1978 edn. pp. 18-19.
5. *Ibid.* pp. 18-20.
6. *Ibid.* pp. 24-25.
7. *Ibid.* pp. 23-24.
8. *Ibid.* p.30.
9. *Ibid.* p.35.
10. *Ibid.* pp. 35-36.
11. Philip P. Wiener (ed.) *Dictionary of the History of Ideas*, New York, 1973, p.468.
12. *Ibid.*
13. Donald E. Brown, *Hierarchy, History and Human Nature*, The University of Arizone Press, Tucson, 1988, p.145.
14. *Ibid.*
15. R.G. Collingwood, *op. cit.* p. 37.
16. *Ibid.* p.39.
17. *Ibid.* p.40.
18. *Ibid.* p.41.
19. *Ibid.* p.42.
20. Who was fiddling when Rome was burning.
21. *Ibid.* pp. 44-45.
22. Brown, *op. cit.* p. 160.
23. *Ibid.* pp. 160-161.
24. *Ibid.* p. 161.
25. T.R. Sharma, *The Concept of History*, pp. 11-12.
26. *Ibid.* p.12.
27. R.G. Collingwood, *op. cit.* p.46.
28. *Ibid.* p.47.
29. *Ibid.* p. 49.
30. *Ibid.* 49.
31. *The New Encyclopedia Britannica,* Vol. 8, p. 948.
32. *Ibid.*
33. Collingwood, op. cit. p.50.
34. *Ibid.* p. 52.
35. Donald E. Brown, *Hierarchy, History and Human Virtue*, p.47.
36. *Ibid.* pp. 47-48.
37. *Ibid.* pp. 51-52.
38. *Ibid.* pp. 53
39. *Ibid.* p.53.
40. *Ibid.* p.54.
41. *Ibid.* pp. 54-55.
42. *Ibid.* p.54; as quoted:

Robert M. Hartwell, *Historical Analogism, Public Policy, and Social Science in Eleventh and Twelfth Century China.* 1971: 694-95; *American Historical Review* 76: 690-727.

43. Philip P. Weiner (ed.) *Dictionary of the History of Ideas*, p.481.
44. *Ibid.*
45. *Ibid.* p. 479.
46. T.R. Sharma, *The Concept of History*, p.14.
47. Brown, *op. cit.*, p. 55.
48. Wiener (ed) *Dictionary of History of Ideas*, p.481.
49. *The New Encyclopaedia Britannica,* 15th edition, Vol.8, p.960.
50. Donald E. Brown, *Hierarchy, History and Human Nature,* pp. 20-21.
51. Romila Thapar, *Ancient Indian Social History,* p.269.
52. A.K. Majumdar, "Sanskrit Historical Literature and Historians" in Guy S. Metrause Francois Gronzet, *Studies in the Cultural History of India* (1st edn.), UNESCO, Agra, 1965, pp. 215-216.
53. Romila Thaper, *Ancient Indian Social History*, pp. 272-273.
54. V.S. Pathak, "Ancient Historical Biographies and Reconstruction of History" in S. Gopal & R. Thapar (eds.), *Problems of Historical Writing in India,* pp. 11-21.
55. Brown, *op. cit.*, p. 23.
56. R.Thapar, *op. cit.*, p.269.
57. *Ibid.*
58. A.K.Warder, *An Introduction to Indian Historiography,* Preface, p. VII cf.
59. Ibid. p.x.
60. *Ibid.* pp. 15-37.
61. *Ibid.* pp. 38-152.
62. Sir Monier Monier-Williams, *A Sanskrit-English Dictionary,* Delhi, 1963, p.165, Col.2.
63. A.K. Warder, *An Introduction to Indian Historiography*, pp. 15-16.
64. T.R. Sharma, *Personal and Geographical Names in the Gupta Inscriptions*, p.98.
65. Edward C. Sachau, *Alberuni's India,* p.308.
66. A.K. Warder, *op. cit.,* p.17.
67. Rigveda X.90. 12-14, Griffith's translation, Delhi, 1999, p. 603.
68. Nirukta II,III-10.
69. *Srimad Bhagvadgita*, IV, 7-8.
70. *Ibid.*, IX. 6; VII, 13-14; XI. 33.
71. Buddha Prakash, *Itihasa-Dharsana*, pp. 1-10.
72. T.R. Sharma, *The Concept of History*, p.79.
73. *The Bhagvadgita,* XVIII. 78.
74. Sri Aurobindo, *The Human Cycle, the Ideal of Human Unity, War and Self-determination,* Pondicherry, Fifth Combined Edition, 1977, p.577.
75. *Ibid.*
76. T.R. Sharma, *The Concept of History*, p.81.
77. *Ibid.*

78. *Ibid.*
79. *Mahabharata*, 3.97.
80. Ma Nisada Pratistham tvam agamasasvatisama yat kraunchamithuna-dekamavadih kamamohitam. Vr: Balakanda, p.6.
81. *Ibid.* p.7.
82. M.R. Kale (ed.) *The Abhijanana-Sakuntalam of Kalidasa,* Bombay, 1961, Introduction, pp. 46-47.
83. Bholashanker Vyasa, *Sanskrit-Kavi-Darshana,* Banaras, 1955, pp. 84-86.
84. R.P. Kangle, *The Kautilya Arthasastra* 1.6. 4-10 (Part II), pp. 12-13.
85. Sachau, *Alberuni's India,* p.404.
86. *Ibid.*, pp. 404-405.
87. *Ibid.* pp. 405-406.
88. Warder, *op. cit.* pp. 17-18. *Arthasastra* I.5.14 : puranamitivrt-tamakhyayikodaharanam I dharmas'asthramarthasastram chetitihasah II.
89. *Arthasastra* I.3.2.
90. T.R. Sharrma, *The Concept of History*, p.13.
91. *Ibid.* p.13.
92. *Ibid.*
93. *Ibid.* p.83.
94. *Ibid.* p.83.
95. Warder, *op. cit.* pp. 18-19.
96. Romila Thapar, *Ancient Indian Social History* , p.274.
97. Tej Ram Sharma, *Research Methodology in History,* p.85.
98. D.C.Sircar, *Indian Epigraphy,* p.18.
99. *Ibid.* pp. 17-18.
100. Tej Ram Sharma, *A Political History of Imperial Guptas*, p.90.
101. D.C. Sircar, *Indian Epigraphy*, p.18.
102. *Ibid.* pp.19-20.
103. *Ibid.* p.23.
104. Tej Ram Sharma, *Personal and Geographical Names in the Gupta Inscriptions*, pp.309-372.
105. D.C. Sircar, *Indian Epigraphy,* pp. 23-24.
106. *Ibid.* p.284.
107. D.C. Sircar, *Selected Inscriptions*, pp. 269 ff.
108. D.C. Sircar, *Indian Epigraphy*, pp. 284-285.
109. *Ibid.* p.285.
110. D.C. Sircar, *Indian Epigraphy* p.285.
111. Tej Ram Sharma, *A Political History of Imperial Guptas*, p.48.
112. *Ibid.*pp. 45-60.
113. Tej Ram Sharma, *A Political History of Imperial Guptas*, pp. 45-60.
114. D.C. Sircar, *Indian Epigraphy*, p.285.
115. Tej Ram Sharma, *op. cit.*, pp. 105-139.
116. K. Krishnamoorthy, *Banabhatta*, Sahitya Akademi, New Delhi, 1976, Second Edn., 1982, p.9.
117. A.K. Majumdar, *op. cit.*, p.216.
118. K. Krishnamoorthy, *Banabhatta*, p.16.

119. *Ibid.* p.14.
120. *Ibid.* pp. 49-50.
121. Warder, *op. cit.* p.38.
122. Guys. Metraux Francots Crouzet, *op. cit.* pp. 217-218.
123. Warder, *op. cit.* pp. 42-43.
124. *Ibid.* pp.218-219.
125. *Ibid.* p.219.
126. G.S.M. Crouzet, *op. cit.*, pp. 219-221.
127. Romila Thapar, *Ancient Indian Social History*, p.276.
128. G.S.M.F., Crouzet, *op. cit.* p.223.
129 *Ibid.*
130. *Ibid.*
131. *Ibid.* p. 222.
132. *Ibid.* p.223.
133. *Ibid.* p.225.
134. Romila Thapar, *op. cit.* p.276.
135. GSMFC, *op.cit.*, p.227.
136. *Ibid.* pp.227-228.
137. *Ibid.* p.226.
138. *Ibid.* p.226.
139. *Ibid.* p.226.
140. *Ibid.* p.227.
141. *Ibid.* pp. 228-239.
142. Romila Thapar, *op. cit.*, p.275.
143. *Ibid.*
144. Warder, *op. cit.*, p.26.
145. *Ibid.*, pp. 27-28.
146. Romila Thapar, *op. cit.* p.278.
147. Warder, *op. cit.* pp. 29-33.
148. *Ibid.* pp. 32-33.
149. *Ibid.* p.33.
150. *Ibid.*
151. Romila Thapar, *op. cit.*, p.277.
152. Warder, *op. cit.*, pp. 278-279.
153. Romila Thapar, *op. cit.* pp. 278-279.
154. *Ibid.* pp.280-281.
155. *Ibid.* p.284.
156. *Ibid.* pp. 286-288.
157. *Ibid.* p.288.
158. *Ibid.* p.289.
159. *Ibid.* pp. 289-290.
160. Paritranaya Sadhunam, Vinasaya cha Duskrtam Dharma. Samsthaparthaya sambhavami Yuge Yuge. II Cf. " Dukha mein simran sabha kare, Sukh mein kare na koye".
161. *Ibid.* pp. 291-292.
162. *Ibid.* p. 292.

163. *Valmiki and Vyasa*, Publications Division, Government of India, New Delhi, 1980, p.39.
164. E.C. Sachau, *Alberuni's India*, p.398.
165. A.D. Pusalker, *Studies in the Epics and Puranas*, Bombay, 1955, p.XX.
166. *Ibid.* p. XXIV.
167. T.R. Sharma, *Research Methodology in History*, p.72.
168. A.D. Pusalkar, *op. cit.*, pp. XXIII – XXIV.
169. *Ibid.* pp. XXV–XXVI.
170. *Ibid.* pp. XXXI–XXXII.
171. *Ibid.* p. 95.
172. *Ibid.* pp. 95-96.
173. *Ibid.* p. 102.
174. *Ibid.* pp. 122-123.
175. *Ibid.* pp. 74-75, 123; Romila Thapar, AIS, p.285.
176. L.S. Seshagiri Rao (Ed.), *Veda Vyasa*, Bangalore, 1974, Second Print 1980, p.40.
177. A.D. Pusalker, *Studies in Epics and Puranas*, p. XXIII.
178. *Ibid.*, p. 57.
179. *Ibid.*
180. Romesh C. Dutt, *The Mahabharata*, Epic of the Bharatas condensed into English Verse, Allahabad, 1944, p.11.
181. *Ibid.*
182. *Indian Inheritance*, Vol. I, Bharatiya Vidya Bhavan, Bombay, 1955, pp. 72-74.
183. *Ibid.* p.76.
184. *Ibid.* p.79.
185. *Ibid.* p.81.
186. *Sanatana-Dharma*, An Elementary Text Book of Hindu Religion and Ethics, The Theosophical Publishing House, Adyar, Madras, 1939, pp. 269-270; *Mahabharata*, Vana-Parvan, XXIX, 12-29.
187. *Ibid.* pp. 273-274, *Mahabharata*, Vana-Parvan, xxxiii, xxxiv.
188. *Ibid.* p.282; Vana-Parvan,XXIX, 12.
189. *Ibid.* p.283; *Mahabharata*, Shanti Parvan, cccv, 18.
190. Cf. *Chandogya Upanishad*, vii.1.2.4: "Itihasa-Puranah Panchamo vedanam" *Mahabharata critical Edition* I. 57.74.
191. *Mahabharata critcal edition* 1.1. 204: "Itihasa-Puranabhyam Vedain Samupbrhamyat".
192. Donald E. Brown, *Hierarchy, History and Human Nature*, Arizona Press, U.S.A., p.23.
193. *Ibid.* pp. 20-30.
194. K.M. Munshi and N. Chandrasekhara Aiyer (eds.) *Indian Inheritance*, Bharatiya Vidya Bhavan, Bombay, 1955, Vol. I, p.81.
195. Seema Burman, Right Words Can HEAL Your Heart, *The Times of India*, Hyderabad, August 25, 2001, p.12.
196. Rgveda Book X.XXXIV.

197. K.M. Munshi and N. Chandrasekhara Aiyer (eds.) *Indian Inheritance*, Bharatiya Vidya Bhavan, Bombay, 1955, Vol. I, p.61.
198. We have a Sanskrit word 'Akhayana' for legend. Hence *'Etihasikas'* should be correctly translated as 'Historians' not as Legendarians, which seems to be erroneous.
199. Lakshman Śarup, *The Nighantu and the Nirukta*, 2.17-20 pp. 31-32.
200. *Ibid.* p.28. N*irukta* 2. 12-13, RV X.98.5.

2

HISTORICAL WRITINGS IN MIDDLE AGES

The medieval historiography continued the conceptions of Hellenistic and Roman historiography. The medieval historian still depends for his facts on tradition, and has no effective weapons for criticizing that tradition. He treats his material from a universalistic pointing view. Even in the Middle Ages nationalism was a real thing; but an historian who flattered national rivalries and national pride knew that he was doing wrong. The great task of medieval historiography was discovering and expanding the divine plan. The historians set their limits to what they wanted to do. They did not care for an accurate and scientific study of history; what they wanted was an accurate and scientific study of the divine attributes, to enable them to determine what must have happened and what must be going to happen in the historical process. The nineteenth century historians had no sympathy for it.[1]

As the unfolding of divine plan, it was now conceived of as the product of human action, human affairs had been dignified. "Accurate scholarship became important, because human actions were no longer felt to be dwarfed into insignificance in comparison with divine plan. Historical thought once more placed man in the centre of its picture... history thus became the history of human passions, regarded as necessary manifestations of human nature." [2] By the beginning of the seventeenth century Bacon was able to acknowledge three great realms of poetry, history and philosophy ruled over by three faculties of imagination, memory and understanding. Collingwood comments that actually, Bacon's definition of history as of memory was wrong because the past only requires historical investigation so far it is not and cannot be remembered. If it could be remembered, there would be no need for historians.

Bacon himself recognized that unremembered history could be reconstructed from data somewhat as, at the same time, natural scientists were using data as the basis for scientific theories, which is as well needed by the historian to supplement the deficiencies of his memory.[3]

The Renaissance history was rooted in human affairs and saw history as the unfolding of the consequences of human will, impulse and action. A more critical evaluation of sources also developed during the Renaissance. Political analysis was also emphasized in particular. There was more consistent use of socio-political analysis in terms of institutional structure, and their functions and also the techniques of writing that allowed the presentation of this analysis in a history[4] had become more sensitive and common and their subjects were more likely to be secular. The vernacular was coming into use, the universal chronicle was going out of fashion and hagiography was in decline. Methodological awareness had developed too… From Otto's time "it was but a short leap to the more definitive dissolution of medieval historiography in Renaissance Italy."[5]

During much of the Middle ages Europe was highly decentralized, and travel between its regions was relatively difficult.[6] While it is now established that technological developments of enormous import took place in medieval Europe, the comparative hostility of the period to the sciences, natural or social, is disputed.

The period between the decline of Rome and the twelfth century, "renaissance" has been called the "dark age" of theoretical science, compared to the earlier achievements of the Greeks and contemporary activities of the Arabs, Latin natural philosophy remained at a rudimentary level.[7] Education tended to be a monopoly of the clergy, which in effect remained a monopoly of the nobility. Divination was not entirely absent but the church was hostile to many forms of divination. A beginning was made in other social sciences as in Otto's discussion of social stratification in Lombardy. At the same time, the beginnings of new concepts of the individual, art and historiography were perceptible in the 12th century and clearly underway in the thirteenth century.

Constantine founded Constantinople as a new co-capital in the fourth century it became the administrative centre of the empire, while Rome remained the capital in the West. The Greek had become the dominant language in the East, while Latin remained dominant in the West. The Byzantines called themselves Romans and retained much of the Roman culture that disappeared in the west. At some point the civilization centred on Constantinople to have a separate designation, Byzantine, its peculiar blend of Greek, Roman and Christian civilizations. Byzantine historiography is judged as "far superior to that of medieval West." It provided stimulus to the Italian Renaissance when works in Greek – hitherto lost in the West but remained preserved in Byzantium – made their way to Western Europe in the late fourteenth and early fifteenth centuries forcefully reminds us of the Byzantine attachment to History. Consequently when Byzantium faced destruction, the Western world began its Renaissance metamorphosis. Thompson states that the Byzantine historians "were better observers and recorder of events than those of the West." The outstanding historian was Michael Pseluss (1018-1078). His *chronographia* is the "outstanding memoir of the middle ages" exhibiting discriminating psychological insight... clear-cut and brilliant characterizations. Another historian Anna Comnena (1083-1148 or later). In Alexiad, she "heralds the series of gifted Byzantine historians who recorded the decline of the empire from the twelfth century"[8] In addition to maintaining the classics of Greek literature, the Byzantines preserved the legal texts in Latin such as the Justinian code.[9]

In Arabian Peninsula, after the founding of the Umayyad dynasty, which was succeeded by the Umayyad dynasty, which was replaced by Abbasids who moved their capital to Baghdad, remaining there until the Mongols sacked it in 1258. Under the Abbasids, Islamic civilization crystallized and reached its zenith. Islam continued to spread with Islam as its religion and Arabic as its language – unified much of the Near East. Muslim historians used contemporary sources extensively, including various kinds of government documents, letters and speeches. Muslim historians showed a keen interest in the human element had to find in Europe before the Renaissance. Eventually it achieved a definite advance in historiography with Ibn Khaldun (1332-1406) with sociological understanding and systematization of historiography,[10] about whom we have discussed at length earlier.

THE RENAISSANCE HISTORIOGRAPHY

The homeland of new historiography was Italy and within Italy Lombardy though Florence gained more importance after some time. Bruni's *History of Florence* (1415-29) has been lauded much as a 'remarkable achievement of the new historical method', which marks the beginning of modern historiography.[11] Even though Thompson favours Machiavelli (1469-1527) as the greatest of all Italian historians, his contribution lies more to political philosophy than to historiography. Everyone agrees to the contribution of Lorenzo Valla (1407-1457) who was "closer than any other author to expressing the attitudes, presumptions, methods and goals of historical scholarship as it would be practiced for centuries."[12] Rather than seeing history it has been stated that historiography in the West deteriorated after the second century A.D. and "remained inferior until the Renaissance" and termed the medieval period to be a 'calamity for historiography'. The medieval historiography had undue concern with myth, forgery, and fabulous genealogy an uncertain grasp of the distinction between real and ideal, combined with some problems in reasoning or in understanding causation; religious authorship a tendency to ignore or distort the history of the pre-Christian era and an absence of the notion of anachronism.[13] Much of the medieval historical writing lacked historical sense, as a result anachronisms abounded. It was mostly written by Churchmen and projected theological concerns. This led to considerable development of hagiography – biographies of the saints. What mattered was not the man but the office he occupied.[14] The rule of logic was not applied to history and it had inherent weakness in the interpretation of facts.

Brown remarks: "In some respects the difference between medieval historiography and that of ancient and modern Europe is one of degree. Some features of medieval histories are good, some biography was written, and some historians of the period do stand out, e.g. Gregory of Tours (539-594), Bede (673-735), Einhard (*c.*770-840) and Otto of Freising (*c.*1113-1158). Gregory of Tours wrote a history of the Franks down to his time, Bede too completed his to his time, Bede too completed his *Ecclesiastical* History of the English of the English people in 731. He produced more than a bare chronicle, more than popular hagiography, Einherd served for decades in the court of Charlemagne; Otto was a careful and critical historian. His major work was: *The Two Cities: A Chronicle of Universal History to the Year 1146*. "Otto may have been an outstanding historian, but clearly historiography was on the mend."[15] By the twelfth century, biography and autobiography, the bulk of Renaissance historical writing was not about the ancient past but rather the Middle Ages and contemporary events. The historians put what they learned from the past to use in matters of more contemporary concern. They thought history as a practical guide for life. Along with the emphasis on moral and practical lessons to be learned from biography and history, an equal emphasis was laid on praise and blame. There is also use of human psychology, one aspect was more or less universal in human nature while other was the specification of the context of human nature, its causes and consequences. Bruni used such notions as greed, revenge, and lust for power, honour, and fear to explain both individual and collective behaviour. Many people, implying that history in the broad sense must have been considered widely useful, wrote familial and personal records of various sorts.[16] These progressive features of Renaissance in Italy later spread to other parts of Europe.[17]

HISTORY OF HISTORICAL WRITING IN MEDIEVAL INDIA

With Medieval India we enter a new genre of history, i.e. medieval chronicles, which were written by contemporary authors who were either court-historians or free-lancers. Some of them came as travellers and wrote about India. Such writing has its own advantages and disadvantages. They had their own prejudice and bias on the one hand and had the benefit of an eyewitness account seen by themselves or ascertained through reliable eye-witnesses or participants. But it is not still easy to find out the truth as their veracity has often been taken as authenticated, their being contemporary accounts. In case of being contradictory, we can only ascertain them through a methodology at our disposal by a common-sense approach. In contrast we ascertain the knowledge about earlier period on the basis of archaeology, epigraphy, coins and some available literary sources. Hence in the present case we ought to know the personal capability of a chronicler, his aims and objectives, his social and political leanings as well as his sources of information and their veracity etc. We attempt to discuss.

We get to know about *Chachanama*, which throws light on the history of the indigenous ruling dynasty of Sind on the eve of the Arab invasion in 711-712. Originally written in Arabic, it was translated into Persian by Muhammad Ali bin Abu Bakr Kufi in the time of Nasiruddin Qabacha, a Turkish slave officer of Muhammad Ghori, who had been appointed governor of Multan and Uchh (Sind) by his master. Chach is the name of a Brahman minister who had usurped the throne who married the widowed queen of his patron. His son and successor Dahir ascended the throne in c. 708 A.D. who faced this onslaught on Sind and perished in the struggle with the whole of his family.[18] Elphinstone found it to be 'a minute and consistent account of the transactions during Muhammad Kasim's invasions and some of the preceding Hindu reigns. It is full of names and places.[19]

Ableruni (*c.*972-1048)

He was born in Khiva, then called Khwarizm. (A Khanate of Turkistan in Central Asia, now part of the USSR).[20] In 1018-19 he accompanied the invading hordes of Mahmud to the Indo-Gangetic valley as a freelance observer. Alberuni stayed back in India for a number of years and travelled extensively in various parts of the country, studied the language, religion and philosophy of the Hindus and wrote the classic account of the country and its people in Arabic entitled *Tarikh-ul Hind* or *Tahqiq* (or *Tahrir*) *ul Hind,* it was translated later into Persian – translated from Persian into English and edited by Edward C. Sachau under the title – *Alberuni's India.*[21] The work by a

Muslim Indologist Alberuni is a primary source of information about socio-religious condition of India from 1017-1030 A.D. Alberuni was a theologian, philosopher, logician, mathematician, astronomer, astrologer, geographer and physician – all rolled into one. The book presents "a deep sociological study, characterized by a rare spirit of enquiry, modern scientific attitude and sympathetic insight."[22] Alberuni himself says: "My book is nothing but a simple historic record of facts".[23] He made extensive use of Sanskrit literature from which he quotes his various statements from *Brahmagupta, Varahamihara, Srimad-Bhagvad-gita,* the *Vayu Purana* and the *Visnu-Purana.* He also quotes from Kapilmuni's *Sankhya Karika* and Patanjali's *Mahabhasya*. It has been pointed out that Alberuni and his native countrymen were as much the victim of Mahmud's oppression as the Hindus of India and this might have inspired Alberuni with sympathy for them if to Mahmud the Hindus were infidels fit to be slain for resisting plunder, to Alberuni they were "excellent philosophers, good mathematicians and astronomers…" He was himself motivated to write this book on India with reference to contemporary and philosophical literature to fill up a gap in the then Arab literature which contained only 'second hand and thoroughly uncritical account of the beliefs of the Hindus.'[24]

His book is a deep sociological study, characterized by a rare spirit of enquiry, modern scientific attitude and sympathetic insight. The world owes to him the first accurate and comprehensive account of Indian literature and religion. He exhibited the rare spirit of enquiry and detachment. His treatment of sources reveals his scientific mind. Alberuni quotes freely from his authorities, and where these seem to exaggerate or to be inaccurate, his citations are followed by some sharp brief commentary, which gives a ceaseless interest to his pages. His treatment to such subjects as astronomy, chronology, geography and astrology, is throughout scholarly, showing extensive reading and precision of thought acquired by a study of exact sciences. His 'masterly criticism' gives him a 'unique position among Eastern writers'. In fact Alberuni's work was 'like a magic world of quiet, impartial research in the midst of world of clashing swords, burning towns and plundered temples' – a spiritual retort to Mahmud's oppression and iconoclasm.[25]

Al'utbi

He belonged to family of 'Utba' (in Persia). Being secretary of Sultan Mahmud himself, he did not accompany his master in his expeditions. His book *Tarikh Yamini* or *Kitab ul Yamini* that covers the whole reign of Sabuktgin and a part of the reign of Mahmud (up to 1020 A.D.), is an original source of information of Mahmud's expeditions. But as he did not accompany it is deficient in accurate topographical knowledge. His attitude, as an orthodox writer is explicit in his statements. Where he sees the order of God in the actions of Sabuktgin and Mahmud: "often times a small army overcomes a large one by the order of God; the friends of God advancing against the masters of lies and idolatry….." "God bestows honour on his own religion and degrades infidelity etc."[26]

Al Baihaqi (*c.* 996-1077)

Al Baihaqi wrote a 'comprehensive history' of the Ghaznavides in thirty volumes – *Tarikh I-Baihaqi* also known as Taj-ul-Futuh (for Mahmud); *Tarikh-I-Masudi* (for Masud) etc. It is more of a gossiping memoir than an elaborate history. But being highly original, its chief merit lies in the minute details, which throw light on the contemporary age – court life, manner of conducting business including the nature of the agenda of the council at Ghazni and the administrative personnel.[27]

Hasan Nizami

Hasan Nizami's *Tajul-Ma'asir* – The crown of Exploits deals primarily with the history of Qutbuddin Aibek. It is the first historical narrative, which deals with the beginning of Muslim rule in India.[28] He projects the early Muslim conquerors as good Muslims and religious zealots whose primary aims and motives in their wars and conquests, government and administrative were religious rather than political or economic and that in all cities and places they conquered, hardly any idol, temple or religious sanctuary was left intact that was not converted into Muslim institutions.[29] He was a panegyrist, like many other historians and suffered from prejudices. He omits to mention Mohammad Ghori's defeat at the first battle of Tarain but refers to restoration of lost prestige at the second battle. However, he hints at the virtual defeat of the Ghurid ruler by Bhimadeva II of Anhilwara earlier.[30]

Minhajus Siraj

Minhajuddin us Siraj of Juzjan (between Merv and Balkh) belonged to a distinguished ancestory. His family had long been in the service of the house of Ghur. He wrote his work, *Tabaqat I-Nasiri* in honour of his patron Nasiruddin and adopted an eulogistic manner in writing it. In methodology he took great pains in collecting information from 'trustworthy chronicles', testimony of persons, hearsay and unspecified sources. Some of his statements are 'too concise to be of much use'.[31] He produced an elaborate history of the Islamic world in twenty-three small but compact volumes or books (*majiladad*), entitled *Tabaqat I-Nasiri*. This work was well-known to the later medieval historians though its wide circulation was suppressed by Mughal emperors because in the last volume (III) he had exposed the Mongol marauders, the destruction wrought by them in Central Asia and the atrocities committed by them on the Muslims.[32]

Amir Khusrau (*c.* 1252-1325)

Amir Khusrau was not a professional historian but has written about half a dozen historical works, including prose chronicles and *masanvis* (poetical compositions). He was the first and a most prominent 'representative of Indo-Muslim culture' of early medieval India. He adorned the courts of all the Sultans from Balban to Ghaisuddin Tughlaq as the poet laureate, was popularly known as Tuti-e-Hind, 'the parrot of India'.[33] His association with the Sultans and the intimate intercourse with the aristocracy, military oligarchy and the saint Nizam-ud-din Auliya gave him the unique opportunity of knowing truth about the political events and social conditions of the time. He was more a poet than a historian, more a panegyrist than an impartial writer.[34] The *Qiran-us-Saadain* (Conjunction of Two Planets, 1285) consisted of several descriptive poems, climaxed by the interview of father (Bughra Khan, ruler of Lakhnauti) and son (Sultan Muiz-ud-din Kaiqubad). The *Khazain-ul-Futuh* or *Tarikh-I-Alai* (in prose), the most reliable and accurate history of first sixteen years of Al-ud-din's reign (conquest of Deogiri to that of Warangal) bears the impress of the author's poetic nature, literary skill, his political opportunism and fondness for India, and everything Indian. It makes use of 'nisbat' (metaphors, similies or allusions, derived from an object) of Quranic verses (to add force and dignity) and chronograms, and of Hindi words. Without referring to the assassination of Ala-ud-din's uncle, Amir Khusrau ascribes Sultan's accession to God's will. His *Afzal-ul-Farwaid* throws valuable light on the saintly character of Nizam-ud-din Auliya and the poet's intimate association with him.

The *Tughlaq-nama*, the last historical poem of Amir Khusrau tells the story of the seizure of Delhi by Ghiyas-ud-din Tughlaq with a religious and moral colour. He did not use evidence of events systematically and critically. He does not indicate the sources of information (except in Diwal Rani). In the final analysis history is unintelligible except as the outcome of divine will or fate.[35]

Zia-ud-din Barani (b. 1285)

He regards history as a science rather as 'the queen of the sciences'. He mentions some advantages of studying history.[36] He has been rated the greatest of all the contemporary historians of early medieval India. His book the *Tarikh-I-Feroze Shahi* preserves the history of the Delhi Sultanate for full one century, from 1259 to 1352. The author started his work just where Minhajus Siraj had left it. His account is not descriptive but analytical and critical; he does not bother about the details; instead he takes up the political and administrative issues as a 'compact whole' and through a manner of scientific presentation, reveals the characteristic of the period to which they belong.[37]

Barani's Fatawa-I-Jahandari is a complementary volume to the *Tarikh-I-Feroze Shahi*. In this book the author explains in historical perspective how the original Islamic theory of kingship and the foreign political institutions adopted by the Turkish rulers of Delhi, underwent radical changes in the Indian setting over the passage of two centuries. The book deals with subjects like powers and functions of the crown, privileges of the mobility, religion and politics, role of the army, and the intelligence services of the Sultans.[38]

It may be mentioned that Sultan Feroze Shah Tughlaq has left a brochure of thirty-two pages in autobiographical writing called *Futuhat-i-Feroze Shahi*, which gives a brief summary of his military campaigns, explains the concept of his kingly duties which was based on religious, humanitarian and moral obligations.[39]

Shams-I-Siraj Afif (b.1354 A.D.)

Another famous historian of the Tughlaq period Shamsi Siraj Afif has also left a standard work entitled *'Tarikh-i-Feroze Shahi'* which is devoted exclusively to the reign of Feroze Tughlaq and constitutes the most accurate and authentic contemporary account of his times. The book is unique in the sense that it also describes the life and condition of the people at large, the one aspect that has usually been ignored by contemporary writers.[40]

The memoirs of Amir Timur (1334-1405) entitled *Tuzuk-i-Timuri* or *Malfuzat-I-Timuri* gives the factual information relating to Timur's destructive activities. A few references to the Indian social life found in the *Tuzuk-I-Timuri* are borne out by '*Zafarnama*' of Maulana Yazdi, a courtier of the Timur house who wrote an account of military exploits in 1424.[41]

Yahya bin Ahmad Sirhindi

Tarikh-i-Mubarak Shahi of Yahya bin Ahmed Sirhindi is the only contemporary source discovered so far on the history of Sayyad dynasty (1414-51). The author had consulted 'various histories' for writing the earlier part of the book while the account of the Sayyads was based upon 'trustworthy' information and personal knowledge. It was consulted and duly acknowledged by the historiographer of the Mughal period, including Nizamuddin Ahmad, Badauni and Firishta.[42]

Khwajah Abdullah Malik Isami (b.1311 A.D.)

Khwajah Abdullah Malik Isami was a scholar and poet of the fourteenth century, wrote an historical *masanavi*, *Futuhus Salatin* in 1349-50 on the Turkish rule in India from the Ghaznavids to Muhammad bin Tughlaq. He explains in detail the circumstances, which led to the foundation of Bahamani kingdom, when Alauddin Hasan extended his patronage to him. The work is not a critical history: it suffers from factual mistakes and omissions of important events.[43] He projects a pre-ordained divine pattern in the course of history and the invisible role of fate too.

The Travelogues

Apart from writers discussed above, we find a few travelogues of the foreigners who visited India during the early medieval period, also throw some light on the political developments.

***Ibn Battuta* (c.1304-78)**

He was Arab traveller from Morocco, wrote his travelogue, entitled *Kitab ur Rehla* (tans. The Rehla of Ibn Battuta) which is a primary source of history of Muhammad bin Tughlaq. It throws light on the socio-political conditions of his times. Abdur Razzak, the author of *Matlaus Sa'dain wa Majmaul Bahrain*, was a Persian scholar. He gives a detailed account of his journey to and from Vijaynagar court and its working, the personal life style of the sovereign and his countries, and the socio-cultural condition of the people of Deccan in general.

We also know of Nicolo Conti, a Venetian, more than a century and half later, visited Southern India. Duarte Barbosa was a Portuguese official in Cochin during *c.*1500-16. He has also written on the Vijayanagar kingdom. Another Domingos Poes visited Vijayanagar kingdom during *c.*1500–02.[44]

However, we cannot omit the mention of two monumental works on historiography in early medieval period, one in India, Kalhana's *Rajatarangini, a chronicle of the kings of Kashmir* in India and the other by Ibn Khaldun: The *Muqaddimah: An Introduction to History* in Arabia.

Kalhana's Rajatarangini

Numerous Hindu states flourished independently of the Sultanate of Delhi who wrote their own history based on indigenous sources. Kashmir was one such a state where Kalhana wrote a chronicle of kings of Kashmir starting from the earliest period down to A.D. 1148-49. It is a general history of Kashmir, not the history of one dynasty only. He was the minister to king Harsha of Kashmir (A.D.1089-1101). He authored the history of Kashmir in eight books in simple Sanskrit verse, in almost eight thousand verses. The mission of a historian, says he, is 'to make vivid before one's eyes pictures of a bygone age.'

In this respect history is more potent then the mythical ambrosia, for while the latter gives immortality to a single individual (who drinks it), a true history immortalizes a number of great men as well as the historian.[45] Kalhana had a highly developed, almost modern, conception of the proper data, or sources of history. He not only made a thorough study of all previous writings on the history of Kashmir, but also consulted the original sources; says he: "By the inspection of ordinances (*sasana*) of former kings relating to religious foundations and grants, laudatory inscriptions (*prasasti-patta*) as well as the written records (*sastra*), all wearisome error has been set at rest". There is evidence to show that he studied coins and old monuments, two other well-known sources of history.[46] He has also painstakingly collected popular traditions associated with places of historical interest. He has also consulted major works written on the regions such as the *Nilamata Purana,* Kshemendra's *Nirpavali,* Helaraje's *Parthavali,* and the *Chavillakara* etc. Of these the *Nilamata Purana* is the most important traditional source on the early history of Kashmir, although it suffers from the same weaknesses as the other Puranic sources. The *Mahattmyas* were another interesting source, being the handbooks of the family priests at various places of pilgrimage. The *Vitastamahatmya*, for example, mentions the important places of pilgrimage along the Vitasta or Jhelum River in Kashmir and relates the historical events (as handed down in tradition) connected with these places. Kalhana's use of inscriptions as source material is a strikingly original element in his historical writing.[47]

He was writing in a period of great stress, civil war and political confusion. He was influenced by the Brahmanical, the Buddhist and to some extent by the Chinese tradition and possibly the Turkish writing of history. The maturity of Kalhana's historical writing is most evident in the last book of the *Rajatarangini* (Book Eight), the quality of analysis is quite different from that of the earlier books since he was writing on a period he was most familiar with. Historical events are now discussed from many points of view – the personalities involved and their ambitions, weakness and power; the emergence of feudatories and their relationship with the king, the role of Damaras and Brahmanas in Kashmir politics, the economic conditions of Kashmir. He recognized the multiplicity of causes, all to his credit. The medieval political history of Kashmir was dominated by two court factions, both of a military nature, the Tantrins and the Ekangas.[48]

Some account is given of the long agony of the struggle of the Sakas of Gandhara with the Turks known as the 'Turkish wars' after an enemy unprecedently bloodthirsty, fanatical and destructive, who aimed at not to conquer the country but to obliterate a civilization.

Supplements were written to Kalhana's work by Kashmiri historians in order to bring the record up-to-date. The most important of these is by Jonaraja in the middle of the 15th century. He was followed by his pupil Srivara who carried the work a little further, beginning with Jainollabhadina (A.D. 420), then at the end of the 16th century Prajyabhata and Suka continued it down to the conquest of Akbar in 1586.[49]

They do not reveal the same grasp of historical process as of Kalhana.[50] Kalhana shows a sound knowledge of geography, of historical detail, and of human character. He provides 'vigorous' biographical sketches, and evaluates even his heroes with that 'spirit of detachment' that will admit both weakness and strengths in the same person.[51] Kalhana, as a great historian, would easily take his place among the very best that the world could show before the nineteenth century.[52]

Now we come to another illustrious historian Ibn Khaldun:

Ibn Khaldun

Ibn Khaldun was an historian of early fourteenth century of 'princely rank', whose more recent ancestors were well connected with the rulers of northwest Africa. He had ultimately Arabian origin too of 'nobility'. His *Muqaddimah* is saturated with a motif of social nobility. He attaches importance to nobility if it is a basis for group feeling otherwise he considers it a 'delusion'. According to him man is the child of customs, not the child of his ancestors.[53] In the *Muqaddimah*, he essayed to provide, comprehensively yet in detail, an understanding of human social organization. As the historian faced with the task of critically evaluating the historical record, he needs it all the more without which it can lead to partisan reporting. But the most powerful cause of error is ignorance of human social organization and culture. A key term used by the author is *asabiyah*, variously translated as *esprit de corps*, group feeling or solidarity. Etymologically, the term derives from the word for paternal kin, and it was generally used in somewhat pejorative sense of clannishness. Ibn Khaldun gave it positive connotation and identified it as a key to political power. In addition to that arising from the ties of kinship, Ibn Khaldun also identified group feeling from territoriality, propinquity, religion, property interests, rank and clientage. He describes at length the conditions that give rise to or diminish group feeling in each of these modes.[54] He sparked a flurry of sophisticated socio-economic historical studies in the fifteenth century Egypt. He well illustrates the connection between historical writing and the social sciences, and considers political matters, always subordinate to religious issues. Ibn Khaldun, the greatest of all Muslim historians, was unquestionably involved in earning good marks for Muslim historiography in sociological understanding. He has been called the 'first critical culture historian' and the 'greatest of early modern sociologists' – titles he richly deserves.[55] Ibn Khaldun's fame rests largely upon the *Muqaddimah*, the introduction to his universal history, which gives special attention to northwest Africa and Muslim Spain, though it coves a much wider area too. It is described by Arnold Toynbee as "undoubtedly the greatest work of its kind that his ever been created by any mind in any time or place … the most comprehensive and illuminating analysis of how human affairs work that has been made anywhere."[56]

He gives much importance to group feeling, which fructifies into political power. His secular analysis of the role of power in society almost certainly had no rival until Machiavelli. He compliments the hardship of desert life for this, which preaches that one must cooperate or perish. City, being a place of luxury the great solvent of the group spirit. He describes the normal stages of group feeling and their normal stages of decline. He was a social psychologist since he correlated changing individual and group psychology with stages in the various cycles of social flow.[57] He also pays considerable attention to the economic factors and a sure grasp of the role played by capital and labour. Because of the emphasis, which he placed on environment and the mode of livelihood in shaping social organization and culture, he has been credited with anticipating the materialist view of history.[58]

For Ibn Khaldun 'political and cultural life was moving in never-ending, always repeated circles. He could see that the things may repeat themselves in the long run, and in essentials, but in particulars of each case, there is much room for variation.

Ibn Khaldun view of history is that man is at the centre of events though he believed in many manifestations of the supernatural. Yet he considered the normal course of events to proceed in accordance with the objective conditions of the environment and in accord with the mundane actions of men. His object of study was the affairs of men. If he had serious flaws as a historian, they were ones he shared with Muslim historians in general. His work was especially well regarded in later Ottoman times.[59]

In addition to his history, he also wrote biography and autobiography. After an audience with the great conqueror

Taimurlane, Ibn Khaldun wrote a 'well-balanced estimate of (his) personality.' His autobiography is "the most detailed in medieval Muslim literature". The work contains fewer details of his early childhood, his family situation, and psychological matters in general that would be desirable, but it has a more personal style than was usual at that time.[60]

Chief Features of Sultanate Historiography

Medieval Muslim historiography reflected mainly two distinct traditions of history writing – Arab and Persian. While Arab historiography had a wide range covering society, institutions, politics and culture, the history of the age; the Persian historiography only projected the history of the rulers, the Persian was a courtly flatterer of his patron.

Early medieval Indo-Muslim historiography grew up in a tradition of Turko-Persian culture and largely bears the impress of dynastic historiography, the authors being either connected with royal courts or solicitors of royal patronage. The Turkish conquests in India in the twelfth and thirteenth centuries stimulated historical writings in Persian.

Secondly, it was a projection of the general Muslim historiography growing up outside India. Dr. Peter Hardy has described the period (1206-1440) as "a colonial period in Indo-Muslim historiography – a period when Muslim historians remained aloof within the 'civil lines' of Muslim historical writings."[61]

Thirdly, the Indo-Muslim historians made history revolve round its 'great man' and deal with political problems and events. Isami was the only writer above fear or favour of the Sultans.[62]

The dynastic periodization was handicapped by the overlapping of events and involved much repetition. Barani confuses dates quite frequently. A different form of history was versified history. Isamis *Futuh-us-Salatin* also suffers from chronological accuracy – at times the dates given are wrong. With the succession of historians, there is an increasing amount of information on the same subjects or different aspects of them. There is little evidence to prove that these authors adopted any definite method of ascertaining of their information by questioning it. They on the one hand reflected, and on the other tried to influence, the ideology of the imperial ruling class or one section of it or the other. They generally advocated explicitly or otherwise, the establishment and continuance of a particular type of state organization wherein a stable relationship would prevail between the Sultan and the nobility. But the Sultanate kept on developing and changing in spite of the historians what they pleaded. It is for this reason perhaps that the general sequence of the historians of the period (except Minhaj's *Tabaqat*) is on the whole critical of the sultans as well as full of denunciation of the world which did not remain stuck where the historians wanted it to. It at least indicates the bias of the historians which colours their narrative.[63]

Chief Features of Mughal Historiography (16th to 18th Centuries)

If pre-Mughal historiography was extra-Indian in inspiration and methodology, Mughal historiography reflected 'a distinctive Indian historical tradition.' It grew up as a result of the 'confluence of three streams', one older and two new.

The Perso-Islamic or Indo-Persian tradition, local and general (or writing general histories as well as regional histories), which continued during the Mughal period and on account of which a definite breach with the past did not take place.[64] While in the earlier period, the histories are more or less impressionistic, by the time Abul Fazl began writing his book, some elements of what is today called research methodology were beginning to be used.[65] The historians generally treat historical events as single, individual events, unrelated to one another, and their narrative style reinforces the singularity of the events. They are a product of human volition. In particular the rulers' nature or will is treated as a major causal factor in the events of his reign. And in the light of their current experience, they explained the occurrence of similar events in the distant or near past also in terms of the operation of human volition.[66] The collation of evidence minus the investigation of the general framework of an informant – whether a book or a person – was also the highest point of development that medieval Indian history writing had reached in the hands of Abul Fazl. It may be noted that medieval Indian approach differs very substantially from the medieval European approach. In the works of medieval European histories most of which were ecclesiasts, historical events are treated, as a manifestation of divine will.[67] The historical writings and semi-historical literature of the Mughal age, some of these served as channels to secularise history writing in the Mughal age.[68]

We also find the influence of the Mongol tradition, a new tradition in historiography by utilizing the vast dynastic archives and other secret and public materials, which were in access to ministers, secretaries or officers. There were more distinctive forms introduced by the Mughals, e.g. official chronicles, memoirs, development of historical biography, official records or court bulletins; royal autobiographies and memoirs, non-official or private histories or historical biographies, biographical literature, gazetteers and correspondence through letters both official and private, administrative manuals or *Dastur ul'Amals*. Then Afghan histories and Hindu historians' writings in Persian in Mughal India constitute a class by themselves.[69]

The general histories of Muslim India by Nizamuddin Ahmad and Abdul Qadir Badauni were the first definite exponents of the new Indian tradition that grew up under the Mughals. In the second place, the official chronicles of particular reigns constituted a novel feature of the Mughal age. Thirdly, the local and regional chronicles for each independent or semi-independent dynasty and each province, though less extensive than the general chronicles, reproduced the main features of Mughal historiography.[70]

The motive of getting a reward or element of personal gain remained in the background or at least was not prominent now as in the previous period. The humanistic aspect of history tended to be more marked and the divine causation less prominent in the Mughal period than in the preceding age. Further the didactic element in history diminished in the Mughal age when historians devoted more attention to events, actions and measures taken, political, administrative or military, and of their causes and effects than general morals or vague warnings. The most significant change was the secularization of history in the

Mughal period. A change is also discernible in the class of writers of historical literature in the Mughal age.[71]

Mughal Historiography

Indian historiography, which has been recognized as an Islamic heritage, reached the zenith of its growth and development during the Mughal period. Babar, the founder of the Mughal rule in India, occupies a place of pride among the contemporary writers, to whom we are heavily indebted for our knowledge of the political, social and cultural conditions of the country in the first quarter of the sixteenth century. His autobiography variously styled as '*Tuzuk-i-Baburi*', '*Waqiat-i-Baburi*' or simply *'Babarnama'* constitutes a first rate authority not only on his own career but also on the socio-cultural history of his times.

'*Tarikh-i-Rashidi*' of Mirza Haider Dughlot is the next most important source of our information about the rise of Mughal power in India under Babar and its subsequent eclipse during the period of Humayun Mirza. Haider Dughlat was a cousin of Babar.[72]

Gulbadan Begum (The Princess 'Rose-body') was a daughter of Babur wrote her reminiscences in the form of a book, entitled, *Humayun Namah* on a request from Akbar.[73] Though not of much value as a political history, it gives an account of Humayun's character.

Khwand Amir also wrote *Qanun i Humayuni*, which informs us about the administrative innovations introduced by the emperor during the early years of his reign.

Jauhar Aftabchi wrote *Tarikh i Humayuni*, which gives us many interesting details about the Emperor's life, especially based on his personal observation.[74]

Abbas Khan Sarwani: Regarding the Afghan rulers – Lodis and Surs, Abbas Khan Sarwani's *Tarikh-i-Sher Shah* gives us information of the administrative achievements of Sher Shah.

Ahmad Yadgar wrote the *Tarikh-i-Salatin-i-Afghana* or the *Tarikh-i-Shahi* in the last quarter of the sixteenth century. It gives us an authentic account of the Lodi and Sur dynasties based on all the literary sources.[75]

Abdullah of Koil (Aligarh) wrote *Tarikh-i-Daudi* in the time of emperor Jahangir. It gives an account of Afghan rulers of India, including the Lodis and Surs.[76]

Niamatullah compiled *Tarikh-i-Khan Jahani* in the reign of Jahangir, which gives a genealogical record of the various Afghan tribes with special reference to the Lodis and the Surs who gained political ascending in medieval India.[77]

Akbar and the Contemporary Historians

Abul Fazl: His '*Akbarnama*' constitutes the main source of our knowledge about the history of Akbar and his times. *Akbarnama* is a monumental work in three volumes; its first volume contains an account of Akbar's ancestors, including that of Babur and Humayun while the second one is devoted exclusively to exhaustive treatment of Akbar's reign in chronological order. The third volume entitled '*Ain-i-Akbari*' is practically a separate work, which throws light on the administrative system and the state policy of the Imperial Mughals and also the inner working of Mughal bureaucracy. Besides this the collection of his letters entitled the '*Ruqat-i-Abul Fazl*' also constitutes one of the authentic and useful sources of information regarding the socio-cultural history of Akbar's times. Similarly the *'Insha-i-Abul Fazl'* or the '*Maktubat-i-Allami*' comprises a collection of official despatches prepared by the learned Prime Minister in his official capacity. After Kautilya's *Arthasastra*, the *Ain-i-Akbari* is the second greatest work of historical significance produced by an Indian, the like of which is hard to find even in the annals of European historical literature.[78]

Abul Fazl adopted a rational and secular approach to the subject. To him the history of India did not consist in the conflict between Hinduism and Islam but rather between the forces of nationalism and regionalism, secularism and religious fanaticism, stability and disintegration. Thus he stands unsurpassed among all the historians of his age.[79]

Mulla Abdur Qadir ibn Mulukshah of Badaon : He is the author of '*Muntakhab ut Tawarikh*', which is a comprehensive history of the Muslim rule in India from the Gaznavids to the fortieth year of Akbar's reign. Badaoni seems to be highly subjective in its bitter criticism of Akbar's favourites and his reforms. According to Muhammad Mujeeb we must not dismiss it as deriving from fanaticism, ingratitude or sheer perversity.[80] He writes as he feels, he is a freelance. He has no idea of pleasing anyone. "He has not searched for facts that were obscure or had escaped the notice of others but has given us something live and vibrant, reflecting him and his age."[81] He has adopted "a general tone of censure and disparagement for Akbar", *albeit* his book conveys a much more favourable impression of the character and achievements of that great monarch than the rhetorical flourishes of Abul Fazl.[82]

Khwaja Nizamuddin Ahmad: He is the author of '*Tabakat i Akbari*' like the *Akbarnama* of Abul Fazl, the *Tabaqat i Akbari* of Nizami is an equally comprehensive work and runs into three volumes. The plan of the work is at once original and unique. He divides the country into nine distinct geo-political regions or units, each called by him as a *tabqa* – Delhi, Multan, Sind, Kashmir, Jaunpur, Bengal, Malwa, Gujarat and the Deccan. Within this regional framework, the author describes the dynastic history of the regional rulers, and their conflict with the Imperial government of Delhi, leading ultimately to the defeat and subjugation of most of them by the Mughal emperors, in their attempt to bring about the political unification of the country. The regional history of Malwa, Gujarat and the Deccan as described by the author, is a positive contribution made by him towards extending the scope of the subject. He informs us that there were about 3200 towns in the Mughal empire out of which 120 were big cities which towards the end of the book he expresses his desire to write a separate history of these towns which obviously he was not destined to do, since his premature death at the age of forty-five.[83]

Muhammad Arif Qandahari: His *Tarikh-i-Akbar Shahi* is a general history of Muslim rule in India from the Ghaznavids to 1579. It is an independent work which does not bear the seal of official approval. He adopted a rational approach to his work voluntarily undertaken by him. He throws light on the Mughal administration in an exhaustive manner. He gives a critical appraisal of Akbar's state policy, which is quite independent of the viewpoints expressed by Abul Fazl or Badaoni.

Inayatullah: His work *Takmiat i Akbarnama* forms a supplement to the *Akbarnama* of Abul Fazl as he picks up the threat where Abul Fazl had left and completed the narrative till the death of the emperor in October 1605. He had succeeded Abul Fazl as the court historiographer of Akbar.[84]

Muhammad Qasim Hindushah alias Firishta: His work *Gulshan-i-Ibrahimi* or simply the *Tarikh i Firishta* is one of the most popular works on medieval Indian history by the contemporary writers. It is a general history of the Muslim rule in India up to the accession of Jahangir. His description of the relations of the Mughal court with the succession states of the Bahamani kingdom of the Deccan is particularly informative and original.[85]

Bayazid Biyat : His write up, entitled the *Tazkire-i-Humayun wa Akbar* gives an incomplete and disjointed account of some events related to the lives of Humayun and Akbar from 1552 to 1591. The incidental information given on the administration; long lists of nobles present on critical occasions are quite useful to the researcher than the so-called history of the two monarchs narrated by him.[86]

Abdul Haq Dihlavi's Tarikh-i-Haqqi : He prepared in 1596-97 gives a bitter criticism of Akbar's religious policy.[87]

Yahiya bin Abdul Latif: His *Muntakhab ut Tawarikh* gives a valuable account of the Mughal rule in India, it was written towards the close of Akbar's reign.[88]

Sheikh Ilahabad Faizi Sarhindi's compilation Akbarnama at the suggestion of his patron and employer Sheikh Farid Bukhari, *mir bakshi* of Akbar is useful, in particular for the history of the concluding years of Akbar's reign.[89]

Historians of Jahangir's Reign

Jahangir: The autobiography of the emperor Jahangir entitled '*Tuzuk-i-Jahangiri*' is by far the most compact and comprehensive record in chronological order of the political and socio-cultural developments of his reign for the first 18 years. The memoirs of Jahangir stand no comparison with those of Babur from the viewpoints of literary merit, objectivity and as an historical document. Jahangir wrote his memoirs with the implicit objective of highlighting his achievements as the worthy successor of Babur and Akbar the Great; he, therefore, presents the official viewpoint or justification of all the royal deeds.[90]

Motamad Khan's Iqbalnama is a general history of Mughal rule in India. It is divided into three parts; part one deals with the history of Timurid dynasty in India up to the death of Humayun; the second part describes exclusively the history of Akbar's reign while the third part, bearing the sub-title *Iqbalnama-i-Jahangiri* gives a detailed account of the reign of Jahangir and the accession of Shah Jahan to the throne. The author holds Nur Jahan primarily responsible for most of the misfortunes of Jahangir, and exonerates prince Khurram from the charge of misconduct against his father. The author is charged with partisanship in the matter.[91]

Muhammad Hadi and Khwaja Kamgar Ghariat Khan also wrote on Jahangir. An unknown author also wrote *Intikhab i Jahangir Shah* which offers an intelligent explanation regarding the standard of revolt raised by Mahabat Khan, which as explained was out of frustration against the highhandedness of Nur Jahan and as a protest against her baneful influence in the affairs of state.[92]

Historians of Shah Jahan's Reign

Three different chronicles, each entitled the *Padshah Nama* and written by Muhammad Amin Qazvini, Abdul Hamid Lahauri and Muhammad Waris respectively, give us a very impressive record of Shah Jahan's reign. The *Shahjahan-Nama*, written by Muhammad Sadiq Khan, constitutes by far the most valuable history of the period after the *Padshah Nama* of Waris.

The author gives an impartial and intelligent criticism of Shah Jahan's lapses, and applauds the services of his Hindu officers to the empire. He has a soft word for those who unjustly suffered at the hands of the emperor and is all praise for 'the Deccanis' who put up tough resistance to the Mughal arms.[93]

Aurangzeb and the Contemporary Historians

The first and last court historiographer of Aurangzeb, Mirza Muhammad Kazim, produced the chronicle of the contemporary history covering the first decade of Aurangzeb's reign, under the title '*Alamgirnama*'. It is full of gross flattery and suppression of all incidents discreditable to Aurangzeb. Nevertheless, the emperor stopped the work and in 21st year of his reign the writing of contemporary history was forbidden altogether. Despite this ban, a brilliant historian Muhammad Hashim *alias* Kafi Khan (*Khufia taur par*: Secretive: the title or Khafi Khan was conferred on Muhammad Hashim humourously by Muhammad Shah *alias Rangila*) continued to write secretly and objectively the contemporary history which covered all aspects of Aurangzeb's activities till his death and even the after-effects of his state policies in his work entitled the '*Muntakhab-ul-Lubab*'. It constitutes by for the most objective and complete history of Imperial Mughals, from Babar to 14th year of Muhammad Shah's reign (1733 A.D.).

During the last years of his reign when Aurangzeb was caught in the whirlwind of revolts and disorders of his own creation, there was a spirit of historical writings throughout the country. '*Nuskha-i-Dilkusha*' of Bhim Sen is especially useful as the primary source of our information regarding the affairs of the Deccan. Similarly, the '*Futuhat-i-Alamgiri*' of Mehta Isar Dass is a first hand authority for much of what happened in Rajputana and Marwar between 1657-98.[94] The *Tarikh-i-Iradata Khan* gives history of the Mughal empire from the close of Aurangzeb's reign to that of Farrukh Siyyar. Similarly the *Ibratnama* of Muhammad Kasim is a well-known chronicle on the aftermath of Aurangzeb's reactionary state policies. The two books bearing the same title: *Tarikh-i-Chaghatai* are written by Muhammad Hadi and Muhammad Shafi Teherani, give a general survey of the Mughal rule in India from Babar to the sack of Delhi by Nadir Shah in 1739.[95]

Literature in Sanskrit, Hindi and Regional Languages

Historical literature in Sanskrit language becomes increasingly available towards the last quarter of the sixteenth century although most of them were secondary compositions based usually on Persian literature. For example, the most popular political history of Akbar's reign written in Sanskrit by Mahesh Thakur entitled *Sarvadesvritant Samgraha*, *Akbarshahi Shringar Darpana* by Padma Sundar give details of Akbar's reign. Amarkavya Vanshavali of Ranccoda Bhatt, written after 1665, describes in verse the dynastic history of Mewar up to the coronation of *rana* Raj Singh. Ranchhoda Bhatt was also the author of a unique Sanskrit inscription called '*Raja Prasasti*' which gives a complete history of Sisodia ruling dynasty of Mewar. *Surjan Charitra Mahakavyam* of *Mahakavi* Chandra Shekar in verse gives the military exploits of Rai Surjan of Ranthambhor.[96]

An exceptional category of Sanskrit literature, produced by the Jain monks of Akbar's reign, constitutes primary source material for an appraisal of Akbar's religious policy in general and his relations with Jain monks in particular. It includes '*Bhanuchandra Charitra*' written by Siddhi Chandra Upadhyaya, *Kriparasa Kosh* of Shanti Chandra, and *Karamchand Vansha Prabandha* by Jai Som Upadhaya. The last one written in 1597, is a eulogy on Karam Chand, a minister of Bikaner state who later took up service under Akbar, was instrumental in introducing Jain monks to the court of Akbar.[97]

In Hindi literature '*Dalpat Vilasa*' though a biographical account of *rai* Dalpat Singh of Bikaner, throws voluble light on the character and personality of Akbar as also his relationships with the Rajput ruling families. The *'Nainsi Khyat'* written by Mehta Nainsi, the minister of Maharaja Jaswant Singh, is a useful history of Rajasthan for the fifteenth and sixteenth centuries with special reference to Jodhpur. It is the only authority for our information about the outcome of Akbar's visit to Nagor in 1570, which resulted in the submission of *rana* Udai Singh of Jodhpur and *rai* Kalyan of Bikaner. Keshava Dass wrote '*Jahangir Chandrika'* but it does not contain any fresh information on the subject.[98]

The Marathi literature, which becomes available from the period of Shah Jahan forms the primary source máterial for the study of factors which led to the rise of the Marathas and the emergence of a sovereign independent state in the South under the leadership of Shivaji. These sources are also indispensable for an objective analysis of the Deccan policy of the Mughals in general and the reign of Aurangzeb in particular. For example, the *Jedha Shakvali* is a chronological table of important events pertaining to the Mughal Empire with exact dates, which has been kept by the Jedhas – a Maratha Kshatriya family, the *Deshmukhs* of Rohit valley in the Maval region of Maharashtra. It contains 243 entries, starting with the birth of Aurangzeb in 1618 A.D. and ending with the second siege of Jinji in 1697 A.D.[99]

The regional historians of the Punjab, and the Sikh studies in particular, have made use of the indigenous literary sources in Gurmukhi script. Of these *Bachittera Natak* by Guru Gobind Singh and *Singhan di Bhagatmala* by Bhai Mani Singh, a disciple and life-long helpmate of Guru Gobind Singh throw light on the history of Sikhs during the Guru period.[100]

Accounts of Foreigners

After the discovery of the sea-route to India *via* the Cape of Good Hope by Vasco da Gama (1497), the Portuguese established and zealously maintained their monopoly of eastern trade for over a century until they received an effective challenge from the Dutch, the French and the English. Revival of European contacts with India through the sea-route opened the floodgates of the subcontinent to the merchants, Christian missionaries, travellers and adventurers. It is impossible to estimate even approximately the number of Europeans who visited India during the period of imperial Mughals. However, some of their documents contain mere secret gossip while many others reflect the racial, religious and national prejudices of the writers. Nevertheless taken as a whole these accounts comprise a unique category of primary source material. Broadly speaking they can be classified into three categories – records of the European factors, travelogues of merchants and adventurers, and accounts of Christian missionaries.[101]

Archaeological Sources

The archaeological sources including the inscriptions, coins, monuments and other antiquities, are of immense value in the reconstruction of the socio-cultural history of medieval India. The inscriptions have been published mostly in the *Epigraphia Indo-Moslemica*, *Epigraphia Indica* and other antiquarian journals. The researches done by John Marshall, Percy Brown, Burgess, Fergusson, Havell, Cousans and host of other specialists in art and architecture give us an insight into the cultural trends of the times.[102]

REFERENCES

1. R.G. Collingwood, *The Idea of History*, OUP, 1978, pp.52-56.
2. *Ibid.* p.57.
3. *Ibid.* p.58.
4. D. Brown, *op.cit.*, p.249.
5. *Ibid.* pp. 188-89.
6. *Ibid.* p. 189.
7. *Ibid.* p.205.
8. *Ibid.* pp. 208-210.
9. *Ibid.* p. 211.
10. *Ibid.* pp. 218-226.
11. Donald E. Brown, *op.cit.* pp. 245-247.
12. *Ibid.* p. 247.
13. *Ibid.*, *op.cit.* p.181.

14. *Ibid.* pp. 182-83.
15. *Ibid.* pp. 184-188.
16. D. Brown, *op.cit.*, pp. 251-262.
17. *Ibid.* p. 303.
18. J.L. Mehta, *Advanced Study in the History of Medieval India*, New Delhi reprint 2001, p.3.
19. J.N. Sarkar, *History of History – Writing in Medieval India*, Calcutta, 1977, p.33.
20. J.L. Mehta, *op.cit.*, p.3.
21. *Ibid.* pp. 3-4. First published Delhi, 1910, Reprinted 1989.
22. J.N. Sarkar in Muhibbul Hasan (ed) *Historians of Medieval India*, p.167.
23. *Ibid.*
24. Jagadish Narayan Sarkar, *History of History Writing in Medieval India*, Calcutta, 1977, p.77.
25. J.N. Sarkar, in Muhibbul Hasan (ed.) *op.cit.*, pp. 167-168.
26. J.N. Sarkar, *op.cit.* pp. 77-78.
27. *Ibid.* p. 78.
28. J.L. Mehta, *op.cit.* pp. 6-7.
29. J.N. Sarkar, *op.cit.* pp. 79-80.
30. *Ibid.*
31. *Ibid.*, pp. 80-81.
32. J.L. Mehta, *op.cit.* pp. 8-9.
33. *Ibid.* p. 9.
34. J.N. Sarkar, in M. Hasan (ed.) *op.cit.*, p.171.
35. *Ibid.* p.172.
36. *Ibid.*
37. J.L. Mehta, *op.cit.*, p.14.
38. *Ibid.*
39. *Ibid.*
40. *Ibid.* p.15.
41. *Ibid.* pp. 15-16.
42. *Ibid.* p.17.
43. *Ibid.*
44. J.L. Mehta, *op.cit.*, pp. 19-22.
45. Verse 3-4.
46. R.C. Majumdar, 'Ideas of History in Sanskrit Literature', in C.H. Philips (ed.) *Historians of India, Paksitan and Ceylon*, OUP, 1967, p.21.
47. Romila Thapar, in M. Hasan (ed.) *op.cit.*, p.1.
48. *Ibid.* pp. 2-5.
49. A.K.Warder, *An Introduction to Indian Historiography*, Bombay, 1997, p.58.
50. Romila Thapar, in M. Hasan (ed.), *op.cit.*, p.9.
51. Donald E. Brown, *op.cit.*, p.26.
52. R.C. Majumdar in C.H. Philips (ed.) *op.cit.* p.21.
53. Donald E. Brown, *op.cit.*, p.236.
54. *Ibid.* p.227.
55. *Ibid.* pp. 226, 229.
56. *Ibid.* p.227; Toynbee, 1959., 21.

57. Donald E. Brown, *op.cit.* p.228.
58. *Ibid.*
59. *Ibid.* pp. 228-229.
60. *Ibid.* p.229.
61. J.N. Sarkar, *op.cit.*, pp. 35-36.
62. *Ibid.* p.36.
63. Harbans Mukhia, *Historians and Historiography During the Reign of Akbar*, New Delhi, 1976, pp.1-40.
64. J.N. Sarkar, *op.cit.*, pp. 36-37.
65. Harbans Mukhia, *op.cit.*, p.171.
66. *Ibid.*
67. Harbans Mukhia, *op.cit.*, pp.171-172.
68. J.N.Sarkar, *op.cit.*, p.37.
69. *Ibid.* pp.37-53.
70. *Ibid.* 53-54.
71. *Ibid.* p.54.
72. J.L. Mehta, *op.cit.*, Vol. II, pp. 32-33.
73. *Ibid.* p.34.
74. *Ibid.* p.37.
75. *Ibid.* p.38.
76. *Ibid.* p.39.
77. *Ibid.* pp. 39-40.
78. *Ibid.* p. 45.
79. *Ibid.*
80. M. Mujeeb in M. Hasan (ed.) *op.cit.*, p.109.
81. *Ibid.*
82. J.L. Mehta, *op.cit.* p.49.
83. *Ibid. op. cit.* p.52.
84. *Ibid.* pp. 52-53.
85. *Ibid.* p.53.
86. *Ibid.* pp. 53-54.
87. *Ibid.* p.54.
88. *Ibid.*
89. *Ibid.*
90. *Ibid.* p.56.
91. *Ibid.* p.58.
92. *Ibid.* pp. 58-59.
93. *Ibid.* p.61.
94. *Ibid.* p.66.
95. *Ibid.* p.67.
96. *Ibid.* p.68.
97. *Ibid.* pp. 69-70.
98. *Ibid.* p. 70.
99. *Ibid.* pp. 70-71.
100. *Ibid.* pp. 72-73.
101. *Ibid.* pp. 75-78.
102. *Ibid.* pp. 79-80.

3

THE MODERN HISTORIOGRAPHY
Approaches and Trends

RISE OF DEBATE IN PHILOSOPHIES OF HISTORY

The spirit of Renaissance gave new openings to the debates on history. By the beginning of the seventeenth century the debates arose in Europe to give a fresh reorientation to history. It had freed itself from the errors of medieval thought but still awaiting to discover new methods and principles for rediscovery of the past. Collingwood had criticized bacon for his equation of history with memory and advocated for the data collection like the scientists to reconstruct the past. Descartes criticized history for events, which it describes never happened exactly as it described them: "And even histories, true though they may be, and neither exaggerating nor altering the value of things, omit circumstances of a meaner and less dignified kind in order to become more worthy of a reader's attention; hence the things which they describe never happened exactly as they describe them and men who try to model their own acts upon them are prone to the madness of romantic paladins and meditate hyperbolical deeds."[1] Descartes raised the issue of the historical skepticism but did not lay down a method or code of rules for historical criticism.

However, it did not discourage historians who accepting it as a challenge tried to work out their own methods for themselves which gave rise to a new school of historical thought which Collingwood labelled as Cartesian historiography on the analogy of the Cartesian philosophy based on systematic skepticism and thorough going recognition of critical principles.

The main idea of the new school was that the testimony of written authorities must not be accepted without submitting it to a process of criticism based on three rules of method.

(1) No authority must induce us to believe what we know cannot have happened, as implicitly pointed out by Descartes.
(2) That the different authorities must be confronted with each other and harmonized.
(3) The rule that the written authorities must be checked by the use of non-literary evidence.

The general tendency of the Cartesian school was termed as sharply anti-historical, even though the historians were now learning to treat their authorities in a thoroughly critical spirit. The powerful new movement of historical thought constituted a refutation of Cartesian philosophy. When the time for attack came, the persons who led the attack were those whose main constructive interest was in history.

Vico was the first one in the early eighteenth century who stated that any idea, however false, may convince us by its seeming self-evidence, and nothing is easier than to think our beliefs self-evident when in fact they are baseless fictions reached by sophisticated argument: What we need is a principle by which to distinguish what can be known from what cannot; a doctrine of the necessary limits of human knowledge.

History, which is emphatically something, made by the human mind, is especially adapted to be an object of human knowledge. Vico regards the historical process as a process whereby human beings build up systems of language, custom, law, government, etc., i.e. he thinks of history as the history of the genesis and development of human societies and then institutions. Collingwood comments that "here we reach for the first time a completely modern idea of what the subject matter of history is".[2] It opposes the problem of skepticism raised by Descartes, the problem of the relation between ideas and things and is thus profoundly anti-Cartesian. For Vico, no such problem could exist in history as it is not concerned with the past as past, it is concerned firstly with the actual structure of society in which we live; the manners and the customs which we share with the people around us. In order to study these we need not ask whether they really exist. Though Descartes apparently does not follow this paradigm but his skepticism was that history is a kind of knowledge in which questions about facts are not distinguishable and the whole point of Descartes' philosophy consists in distinguishing those two types of questions, remarks Collingwood.[3]

Vico was more interested in the history of remote and obscure periods, that is, in the extension of historical knowledge; and he prescribed certain rules of method:

(1) He talks of certain periods of history having a general character, colouring every detail, which appeared in other periods so that we can analogically describe from one to other, e.g. the Homeric period of Greek history and the European Middle Ages both of them are called by the generic name of heroic periods. To learn more than Homer can tell us about the Homeric age, we should study the middle ages and try to apply to early Greece.[4]

(2) Vico showed that these similar periods tended to recur in the same order which he puts up in a cyclic way: first, the guiding principle of history is brute strength, then valiant or heroic strength; then valient justice; then brilliant originality; then constructive reflection; and lastly, a kind of spendthrift and wasteful opulence which destroys what has been constructed. He is aware that such scheme is too rigid not to admit of countless exceptions.[5]

(3) Thirdly, this cyclical movement is not a mere rotation of history through a cycle of fixed phases; it is not a cycle but a spiral; for history never repeats itself but comes round to each new phase in a form differentiated by what has gone before. That the historian never prophesises.[6]

Vico guards historians against certain prejudices. He categorizes five from these sources of error[7]:

(1) Historian should avoid giving magnificent opinions about antiquity, i.e. the prejudice in favour of exaggerating the wealth, power, grandeur etc. of the period, which the historian is studying.

(2) The conceit of nations. Every nation in dealing with its own past history has a prejudice in favour of painting it in the most favourable colours.

(3) The conceit of the learned. The historian takes the people about whom he is writing as scholars and of reflective intellect. Actually Vico held, the most effective men in history have been the least academically minded. Historical greatness and reflective intellect are very rarely combined. The scale of values, which governs the historian's own life is very different from that which governed the life of his chief characters.

(4) The fallacy of sources or what Vico calls the scholastic succession of nations. This error consists in thinking that when two nations have a similar idea or institution one must have learnt it from other. Rather it depends on the denying the original creative power of the human mind, which can rediscover ideas for itself without learning them from another.

(5) Lastly, there is the prejudice of thinking the ancients better informed than us about the times that lay nearer to them.

Vico is not content with negative warnings. He suggests certain methods by which the historian can transcend mere reliance on the statements of authorities[8]:

(1) He emphasizes the importance of linguistic study, which can throw light on history. Etymology can show what kind of life a people was leading while its own language was coming into existence. Their stock of words shows what their stock of ideas was.

(2) He emphasizes a similar use of mythology. The gods of primitive religion represent a semi-poetical way of expressing the social structure of people who invented them. Thus in Greco-Roman mythology, Vico saw a representation of domestic, economic and political life of the ancients. These myths were the way in which a primitive and imaginative mind expressed to itself what

a more relective mind would have stated in codes of law and morality.

(3) He propounds a new method of using tradition. All traditions are true, but none of these mean what they say; in order to discover what thy mean, we must know what kind of people invented them and what such a kind of people would mean by saying that kind of thing.

(4) In order to find the key to this interpretation we must keep in mind that at a given stage of development will tend to create the same kind of products. Savings, at all times and in all places, are savages in mind, by studying modern savages we can learn what ancient savages were like, and thus find out how to interpret the savage myths and legends that conceal the facts of remotest ancient history. Children are savages of the kind, and children's fairy tales may help in the same direction. Modern peasants are unreflective and imaginative persons, and their ideas throw light on the ideas of primitive society; and so forth.

Thus Vico has drawn our attention to make historical thought constructive as well as critical cutting it loose from its dependence on written authorities and making it genuinely original or self-dependent. He has developed the philosophical principles where he can deliver a counter-attack on the scientific and metaphysical philosophy of Cartesianism. Collingwood calls him too ahead of his time as he was recognized more in the late eighteenth century when there was great blossoming of historical studies in Germany. German scholars rediscovered Vico and his doctrine that ideas are propagated not by diffusion like articles of commerce, but by independent discovery by each nation of what it needs at any given stage in its own development.[9]

The second effective attack on Cartesianism was delivered by the Lockian school culminating in Hume. The Cartesianism had banished history from a place on the map of knowledge. The Lockian philosophy became popular in France and was adopted by the men of Enlightenment, Voltaire and the Encyclopaedists whose interests were definitely oriented towards history which is evident in the Lockian philosophy, though anti-Cartesian but makes a positive contribution in the direction of history, as pointed out by Collingwood.[10]

(1) The denial of innate ideas and the insistence that knowledge comes through experience.
(2) The denial of any argument intended to bridge gulf between ideas and things.
(3) The denial of abstract ideas and the insistence that all ideas are concrete. It is natural way of thinking about history, where knowledge consists not of abstract generalizations but of concrete ideas.
(4) The conception of human knowledge as falling necessarily short of absolute truth and certainty, but capable of attaining (in Locke's words) such certainty as our condition needs; or (as Hume puts it) that reason as incapable of dispelling the clouds of doubt, but the Nature herself (our human nature) suffices for that purpose and lays upon us in our practical life an absolute necessity to live and talk and act like other people.

Collingwood quotes two examples from Hume's *Treatise of Human Nature*, one of the assassination of Caesar in the senate-house on the ides of March, which was a fact established on the unanimous testimony of historians who agreed to assign this precise time and place to that event. The second is the statement that this is contrary to commonsense that the evidence of ancient history does not thus decay with more length. Further that:

> *Though the links are innumerable... depend on the fidelity of printers and copists... After we know one, we know all of them; and after we have made one, we can have no scruple as to the rest.*[11]

Thus Hume had reflection on the problems of historical thought and had shown that Cartesian objectives to it were invalid. As a writer of history Hume ranks with the men of Enlightenment.

Thus we see that Renaissance led to Enlightenment and Enlightenment led to Romanticism, which brought us to the threshold of scientific history that led to Positivism.

The Enlightenment

Hume and Voltaire belong to the school of the historiography of the enlightenment. By the enlightenment, *Aufklarung* is meant that endeavour, so characteristic of the early eighteenth century, to secularise every department of human life and thought which was revolt against religion as such, which Voltaire considered as a function of what was backward and barbarous in human life. Vico thinks of art, religion and philosophy as three different ways in which human mind exposes itself.[12] They have a dialectical succession in a definite order. It follows that a religious attitude towards life is destined to be superseded by a rational or philosophical one though Voltaire or Hume did not formulate any such theory. The historical outlook of the enlightenment was not genuinely historical; in its main motive it was polemical and anti-historical.[13] Voltaire openly proclaimed that no securely based historical knowledge was attainable for events earlier than the close of fifteenth century. In economic terms it meant the spirit of modern industry and commerce. In political terms it meant the spirit of enlightened despotism.

Montesquieu tries to explain the features of a civilization by reference to geographical facts. What determines its character is not the facts of that environment but man is able to get out of them and that depends on what kind of man he is.[14] Gibbon, on the other hand, finds the motive force in history in human irrationality itself and his narrative displays what he calls the triumph of barbarism and religion. Thus Gibbon places his narrative in a golden age when human reason ruled over a happy world, the Antonine period. This conception of a golden age in the past gives Gibbon a rather special place among enlightenment historians and assimilates him on the one hand to his predecessors, the humanists of the Renaissance, and on the other to his successors, the Romantics at the close of the eighteenth century.[15] The central point of history, for these writers, is the sunrise of the modern scientific spirit. Before that everything was superstition and darkness, error and imposture. There is no rational or necessary development in them, the story of them is a tale told by an idiot full of sound and fury, signifying nothing.[16]

The Science of Human Nature

Hume's attack on spiritual substance was the philosophical forerunner of scientific history because it destroyed the last vestiges of the substantialism in Greco-Roman thought. In the introduction to his *Treatise of Human Nature*, he explains the project of his work by stating that "all sciences have a relation, greater or less to human nature, and however wide any of them may seem to run from it, they still return back by one passage or another." Even *Mathematics*, *Natural Philosophy*, and *Natural Religion* (i.e., the three Cartesian sciences – mathematics, physics and metaphysics) "are in some measure dependent on the science of Man: since they lie under the cognizance of men and are judged by their powers and faculties". Consequently, "the science of man is the only solid foundation for all the other sciences."[17]

Men like Bacon had pointed out that improved knowledge of nature would give us improved power over nature, and this was quite true. Assuming human nature to be constant, the 18th century philosophers made it impossible for themselves to arrive at the conception of a history of human nature itself. The same error gave them a false view not only of the past but also of the future, because it made them look forward to a utopia in which all the problems of human life should have been solved. Thus the eighteenth century conception of progress was based on the same false analogy between knowledge of nature and knowledge of mind; though the human mind comes to understand itself better, it thereby comes to operate in new and different ways.[18]

Romanticism

For any further progress in historical thought, first the horizon of history had to be widened through a more sympathetic investigation of those past ages which the enlightenment had treated as barbaric and left them obscure, and secondly, the conception of human nature as something uniform and unchanging had to be attacked. Herder completed these tasks, especially the first one by the work of Rousseau, whereby the whole of human history was to be seen if not as the history of human reason, at least as the history of human will, the general will as Rousseau conceived it had always existed and had always been operative. Thus the tendency of the enlightenment to care only for the present and the most recent past was counteracted, and people were led to think of the past as all worthy of study and all of a piece. The scope of historical thought was thoroughly widened, and historians began to think of entire history of man as a single process of development from a beginning in savagery to an end in a perfectly rational and civilized society.[19]

Herder

Herder who published four volumes about his new attitude to the past (1784-1791), saw human life as closely related to its setting in the natural world. He conceived the general character of this world is that of an organism so designed as to develop within itself higher organisms. He starts with vegetable life whose higher form is animal life and human life is a further specialization of animal. He takes human nature as the perfection of plant nature; Herder explains, sexual love in man is really the same thing as the flowering and fruiting of plants, raised to a higher power.[20]

Herder further divides man, as a natural being into various races of mankind and favours Europe for possessing a historical life, where as in China or India or among the natives of America there is no true historical progress but only a static unchanging civilization with no cumulative development or historical progress.[21] Collingwood remarks that Herder was not a cautious thinker and was not critical of his own ideas. He does not agree with Herder that Europe as the only country that has a history, though we may agree that Europeans had much historical knowledge when Herder wrote. Collingwood also cautions that Herder's doctrine of the differentiation of races should not be accepted without scrutiny, though he is in agreement with Herder that there are differences between different kinds of men, and that human nature is not uniform but diversified. Herder, according to Collingwood, is thus the father of anthropology meaning by that the science which a distinguished various physical types of human beings, and (be) studies the manners and customs of these various types as expressions of psychological peculiarities going with the physical ones.[22] Instead of the Enlightenment's conception of a single fixed human nature we now here the conception of single fixed human nature we now have the conception of several fixed human natures. Today we only know it as a sophisticated excuse for national pride and national hatred. Though it was a pernicious doctrine it showed a clear distinction between nature and man, which was taken up by Kant.

Kant

Kant propounded the view that though moral laws determine human acts yet as phenomena they are determined according to natural laws as the effects of causes. History, narrating the course of human actions, deals with them as phenomena, and therefore sees them as subject of natural laws. Historical actions are not necessarily the records of human wisdom but far more a record of human folly, vanity and wickedness. So Kant gives credit to a plan of nature by seeing a general progress in the life of mankind. The events of history do not 'pass in review' before the historian; he has to re-create them inside his own mind, re-enacting for himself so much of the experience of the man who took part in them.[23]

The plan of nature as Kant elaborates is development of moral freedom, which is the final key to his conception of history. Man is to profit by the work already done by others. No one can invent the whole of mathematics out of his own head. Man is an animal that has the peculiar faculty of profiting by the experience of others; and he has this faculty because he is rational, for reason is a kind of experience in which this is possible.[24]

Collingwood thus remarks that Kant has here achieved the remarkable feat of showing why there should be such a thing as history; "it is, he shows, because man is a rational being, and the full development of his potentialities therefore requires an historical process".[25] Further Kant says that the irrational and immoral elements of pride, ambition and greed, the evil elements in human nature make the continuance of a stagnant and peaceful society impossible. This created a conflict between two motives, which sway human mind. One, a social motive, desire for a peaceful and friendly life, the other an anti-social motive, a desire to domineer over and exploit his neighbours.[26] This restlessness is the means by which nature uses to bring about the advancement of human life. Kant sounds a pessimistic view by stating that the spectacle of human history is in the main a spectacle of human folly, ambition, greed and wickedness, and that any one who goes to it for examples of wisdom and virtue, will be disappointed.[27] Collingwood further comments on Kant that the exaggerated division of history into a wholly irrational past and wholly rational future in the legacy which Kant inherits from Enlightenment. Actually what brought progress not share badness but the concrete activity of human effort itself, with all its good and bad elements comingled.[28] Kant wanted to write a universal history, which could be done by coordinating two disciplines of history and philosophy by a scholar. It exhibits *progress*. It shows human rationality and the means by which it is being brought into existence is human irrationality, i.e. passion, ignorance, selfishness. Collingwood remarks that antithesis is too rigid. "Passion and ignorance have certainly done their work and an important work in past history, but they have never been mere passion and mere ignorance; they have been rather a blind and blundering will for good and a dim and deluded wisdom".[29]

Schiller

He reinterprets Kant's philosophy of history by bringing to it the experience of a working historian. He distinguishes between a professional researcher with his dry-as-dust attitude towards the bare facts which are the dry bones of history, a man whose aim is to know more and more about less and less and thus to become a specialist. The other is the philosophical historian who takes all history for his province and makes it his business to see the connections between the facts and detect the large-scale rhythms of historical process which is really the method of the Romantic school who sympathetically to get inside the facts he is studying. Universal history, so conceived, is the history of progress from savage beginnings to modern civilization.[30] The only difference is that Kant places the goal of progress in a future millennium, Schiller places it in the present and asserts that the ultimate aim of universal history is to show how the present, with such things as modern language, modern law, modern social institutions, modern clothing, and so forth, came to be what it is. Secondly, Kant restricts the task of history to the study of political evolution, Schiller includes it in the history of art, of religion, of economics and so forth and here again he improves on Kant.[31]

Fichte

Fichte agrees with Schiller and disagrees with Kant in conceiving the present as the focal point in which the lines of historical development converge; the fundamental task of the historian is to understand the period of history in which he lives. Every age is the concrete embodiment of a single idea or concept. Every concept has a logical structure involving three phases: thesis, antithesis and synthesis.[32] Fichte is trying to periodize history and attempts to detect a conceptual scheme underlying the temporal succession of historical periods.[33] "The fruits of this Fichtean discovery ripened in Hegel."

Schelling

Schelling gave a more systematic development to the ideas of Kant and Fichte. According to Schelling whatever exists is knowable, two great realms of the knowable are Nature and History. As the process of self-knowledge advances, new stages in self-knowledge enrich the knowing mind and thus create new things for it to know. History is a temporal process in which both knowledge and the knowable are progressively coming into existence, and this is expressed by calling history the self-realization of the Absolute, where the Absolute means both reason as the knowable and reason as the knower.[34]

Hegel

Hegel's philosophy of history is drawn by him from his predecessors, but he has combined their views with extraordinarily skill into a theory so coherent and so unified that it deserves independent consideration as a whole. In his *Philosophy of History*, lectures delivered in 1822-23 where he made history philosophical than mere empirical, that is, history not merely ascertained as so much fact but understood by apprehending the reasons why the facts happened as they did. This philosophical history will be a universal history of mankind (here Hegel follows Herder) and will exhibit a progress from primitive times to the civilization of today. The philosophical history has to answer the question how the state came into existence (all this is taken from Kant). But the historian knows nothing of future; history culminates not in a future utopia but in the actual present (this is Schiller).[35] Man's freedom is the same thing as his consciousness of his freedom, so the development of freedom is a development of consciousness, a process of thought or logical development, in which the various necessary phases or moments of the concept are successively achieved (this is Fichte). Lastly, philosophical history exhibits no merely human process but a cosmic process, a process in which the world comes to realize itself in self-consciousness as spirit (this is Schelling).[36]

According to Hegel, nature is cyclical. Each sunrise, each spring, each tide is like the last, the law governing the cycle does not change as the cycle repeats itself. History, on the contrary, never repeats itself; its movements travel not in circles but in spirals, and apparent repetitious are always differentiated by having acquired something new.[37]

Since Darwin's doctrine of evolution has been accepted by us we are obliged to conceive that the process of nature as resembling the process of history. Collingwood criticizes Hegel for ignoring Darwin but at the same time supports Hegel in stating that it remains true that the process of nature is different from the process of history. For example the succession of geological periods is not a truly historical succession – because it is peculiar to history that the historian re-enacts in his own mind the thoughts and motives of the agents whose actions he is narrating, and no succession of events is an historical succession unless it consists of acts whose motives can, in principle at least, be thus re-enacted.

Secondly, all history is not history of thought. Some actions are merely events, the historian cannot understand them; strictly he cannot even ascertain that they have happened. They are only knowable to him as the outward expression of thoughts. Supporting Hegel, Collingwood states that it is not knowing what people did but understanding what they thought that as the proper definition of the historian's task. Thirdly, the force which is the mainspring of the historical process (to use Kant's phrase) is reason. Supporting Hegel again Collingwood states that everything that happens in history happens by the will of man and the will of man is man's thought expressing itself outwardly in action. Hegel maintains the admitted fact that human history exhibits itself, as a display of passions does not prove that it is not controlled by reason. But all the same, it is a display of reason, for reason uses passion itself as its tool in bringing about its ends, remarks Collingwood.[38] So when it is said that Hegel's view of history is a rationalistic view, it concerns irrational elements as essential to reason itself. However, Hegel insists that historian must first work empirically by studying documents and other evidence. Collingwood remarks that Hegel should have held that historian's business is to study not so much the process of objective mind as the history of absolute mind, i.e. art, religion and philosophy as half of Hegel's collected works is devoted to study of these three things.[39]

Hegel and Marx

Collingwood remarks that Marx's view of history has both the strength and the weakness of Hegel's: its strength, in penetrating behind the facts to the logical nexus of underlying concepts; its weakness, in selecting one aspect of human life (in Hegel the political, in Marx the economic) as in this sense fully rational by itself. Marx, like Hegel, insisted that human history is not a number of different parallel histories, economic, political, artistic, religious, and so on but one single history.[40] But like Hegel, again, he conceived this unity not as an organic unity in which every thread of the developing process preserved its own continuity as well as its intimate connection with others, but as a unity in which there was only one continuous thread (in Hegel, the thread of political history, in Marx that of economic history), the other factors having no continuity of their own but being, for Marx, at every point, in their development saw mere reflections of the basic economic fact. "This committed Marx to the paradox that if certain people held, for example, certain philosophical views, they had no philosophical reasons for holding them, but only economic reasons. Historical studies of politics, of art, of religion, of philosophy, constructed on this principle, can have no real historical value; they are mere exercises in ingenuity."[41]

The Marxian paradox can best be illustrated by reference to his attitude to Hegel's dialectic. The materialism on which Marx so strongly insisted was not ordinary eighteenth century materialism it was 'dialectic materialism'. Dialectic materialism was still materialism – whereas Hegel had broken away from the historical materialism of the eighteenth century, Marx went back on this demand and subjected history once more to that dominion by natural science from which Hegel had proclaimed it free. That is one reason why dialectic materialism has always had its greatest successes with political and economic history, and its greatest failures in the history of philosophy. The conditions, which justified, and indeed necessitated, them no longer exist.[42]

POSITIVISM

The historical materialism of Marx and his colleagues exercised little immediate influence on historical practice, which eventually influenced the implementation of positivism as philosophy of history in the nineteenth century. The positivistic historiography drew its inspiration from the natural sciences. They thought it consisted of two things: first, ascertaining facts; secondly, framing laws. The historians engaged themselves zealously as a first step to ascertain all the facts they could. The result was a vast increase in historical knowledge by compilation of vast masses of carefully sifted material, like the calendars of close and patent rolls, the corpus of Latin inscriptions, new editions of historical texts and sources of every kind, and the whole apparatus of archaeological research.[43] Earlier Hegel had rejected the idea of evolution, regarded differences between higher and lower organisms as logical, not as temporal. But with the publication of *The Origin of Species* in 1859 by Darwin, the conception of nature as a static system changed overall disbelieving that all species were special creations and had long been superseded by the conception of species as coming into existence in time-process. Darwin not only believed in evolution, but that he held it to be brought about by what he called natural selection, a process akin to the artificial selection by which man improves the breeds of domestic animals. Thus the old idea of nature as a static system had been abandoned. This idea gave a green signal to the Positivists to work on history on the analogy of natural science. Evolution could now be used as a generic term covering both historical progress and natural progress.[44]

The positivists did not realize that in science the facts are directly observed by the scientist who can even repeat the experiment if needed. In science thus the facts are empirical facts, facts perceived as they occur. In history, the word 'fact' bears a very different meaning. It is never immediately given. "It is arrived at inferentially by a process of interpreting data according to a complicated system of rules and assumptions. A theory of historical knowledge would discover what these rules and assumptions are, and would ask how far they are necessary and legitimate. All this was entirely neglected by the positivistic historians, who never asked themselves the difficult question: How is historical knowledge possible? How and under what conditions can the historian know facts which, being now gone beyond recall or repetition, cannot be for him objects of perception? They were precluded from asking this question by their false analogy between scientific facts and historical facts… they were all the time misconceiving the nature of historical facts, and consequently distorting the actual work of historical research."[45]

Auguste Comte (1798–1857), who between 1830 and 1842 had written his magnum opus, *Cours de Philosophie Positive* stated "there should be a new science called Sociology (he preferably called it Social Physics) which was to begin by discovering the facts about human life (this being the work of historians) and then go on to discover the causal connexions between these facts. The sociologist would thus be a kind of super-historian, raising history to the rank of a science by thinking scientifically about the same facts about which the historian thought only empirically."[46]

According to Professor Ravinder Kumar[47] who states that the imperialist historians had already done sufficient harm to Indian history, in the nineteenth century, a great damage was done by the positivistic historiography. He severely criticised such historians by quoting illustrations from their works that followed the dwarfed discipline of history from England where it came straight from Germany. He has strongly advocated for the rejection of positivistic historiography, which remained only in the first stage of collecting facts but evaded the second stage of forming laws. Finally, we can say that it only helped history in building up a vast source material in various forms but failed to give a complete philosophy or method to the discipline of history.

After complete rejection of the positivistic historiography, Ravinder Kumar tried to suggest as an alternative in the use of *Varna-Jati* scheme of social organization to employ in the analysis of Indian history. But happily he withdrew it calling it a misleading guide to a reconstitution of our proximate historical past and declaring it even more inadequate a guide to our present.[48] It could eventually lead to the communal interpretation of history, community being the larger representative of *Varna-Jati* scenario, which could only be a retrograde step of interpreting history in modern phenomena.

Actually Collingwood being disappointed by the vulnerable influence of Positivistic historiography culminating into distortion of historical research, was trying to find out a solution to the problem. One needs great patience for going through Collingwood's search for 'a genuinely scientific and therefore autonomous method in historical study'.[49] He tried to find out in England by studying the works of F.H. Bardley: *The Presuppositions of Critical History* written in 1784, the works of

Robert Flint on the philosophy of history in a number of volumes between 1784 and 1803, Miss L. Susan Stebbing: *A Modern Introduction to Logic*, (edn.2) London, 1933 as well as the late nineteenth century historiography for example Freeman's book on *The Methods of Historical Study*, London, 1886, Robert Mackenzie's: *The Nineteenth Century – A History*, published in 1880, Huxley's on *Evolution and Ethics* in 1893, J.B. Bury's *History of Greece*, *The Idea of Progress* and *A History of Freedom of Thought*, M.J. Oakeshott's *Experience and its Modes*, Cambridge, 1933 and Professor Arnold Toynbee's great *Study of History* (which represents a restatement of the positivistic view itself, as pointed out by Collingwood).[50] In Germany the works of Windelband, Rickert, Simmel, Dilthey, Meyer and Spengler (about which Collingwood feels that the conception of culture is openly positivistic)[51]; in France about the works of Ravaisson, Lachelier, Bergson and some other works for which he gives the sub-title: *Modern French Historiography*. In Italy he quotes Croce's essay of 1893 which he discusses thoroughly and Croce's work of 1912 and 1913 and finally Collingwood calls it a special type of pseudo-history which Croce calls philological history. Collingwood tried to find his ideal in the works on history and philosophy of history in England, Germany, France and Italy to the close of nineteenth century and the beginnings of twentieth century. It seems he was not fully satisfied and then wrote an *Epilegomena* which has been published in his work '*Idea of History*' as Part V, where he dilates upon *Human Nature and Human History* as his sub-title under which he discusses (i) The Science of human nature, (ii) History as knowledge of mind[52]and then gives his conclusions in a vivid and detailed manner, where he gives great insights to the reader for Historical Method which he sub-titles as *The Historical Imagination*.[53] Finally, Collingwood comes to grip with *Historical Evidence* when after discussing the evidence he talks of *History as Inferential, Different Kinds of Inference, Testimony* and in the end he criticizes the *Scissors and Paste* method of history. He also discusses about *Historical Inference, Pigeon-holing, Statement and Evidence, Question and Evidence* and finally, *History as Re-enactment of Past Experience, The subject-matter of History, History and Freedom*. It is the

Progress as created by Historical Thinking where Collingwood ends his *Epilegomena*.

With a great compliment to R.G. Collingwood I read all the sections mentioned above with a lively interest and do not deliberately summarize them so as to persuade the reader to go through by himself for larger benefits and great dividends due from him in historical research. These insights are like seeds, which are sure to take the form of big trees if further, deliberated by the readers. We feel highly obliged to R.G. Collingwood for his great effort made in understanding of history as a discipline.

There are further debates in history which do not minimize the work of history but make it a more rewarding and revealing discipline which is not its weakness but strength. With cultural relativism and post-modernism the more schools of thought have entered the domain of history, which is a subject matter for a separate volume for a fair and thorough treatment to most recent and new approaches to history in the 20th century and new century, i.e. 21st century which has opened up new challenges to the domain of history.

REFERENCES

1. R.G. Collingwood, *op.cit.*, p.59.
2. *Ibid.* p.65.
3. *Ibid.* p.66.
4. *Ibid.* p.67.
5. *Ibid.*
6. *Ibid.* pp. 67-68.
7. *Ibid.* pp.68-69.
8. *Ibid.* pp. 69-70.
9. *Ibid.* p.71.
10. *Ibid.* pp. 72-73.
11. *Ibid.* p.75.
12. *Ibid.* p.76.
13. *Ibid.* p.77.
14. *Ibid.* p.79.
15. *Ibid.* p.79.
16. *Ibid.* p.80.
17. *Ibid.* pp. 82-83.
18. *Ibid.* pp. 84-85.
19. *Ibid.* pp. 86-88.
20. *Ibid.* p.89.
21. *Ibid.* p.90.

22. *Ibid.* pp. 90-91.
23. *Ibid.* pp. 96-97.
24. *Ibid.* p. 98.
25. *Ibid.*
26. *Ibid.* pp. 100-101.
27. *Ibid.* p.101.
28. *Ibid.* p.102.
29. *Ibid.* p.104.
30. *Ibid.* pp. 104-05.
31. *Ibid.* p. 105.
32. *Ibid.* p. 106.
33. *Ibid.* pp. 106, 109, 111.
34. *Ibid.* pp.111-113.
35. *Ibid.* p.114.
36. *Ibid.*
37. *Ibid.* pp. 114-115.
38. *Ibid.* p. 116.
39. *Ibid.* p.121.
40. *Ibid.* p.123.
41. *Ibid.*
42. *Ibid.* p.126.
43. *Ibid.* pp. 126-127.
44. *Ibid.* pp. 128-129.
45. *Ibid.* p. 133.
46. *Ibid.* p.128; cf. Francis Abraham and John Henry Morgan, *Sociological Thought*, Madras, 1985, Reprinted 1996, p.12.
47. Prof. Ravinder Kumar, "Social Theory and the Historical Perception of Modern India" in *Modern India*: Presidential Address, IHC, Bombay, 1980, pp. 415-434.
48. *Ibid.* pp. 424-42.
49. R.G. Collingwood, *op.cit.*, pp. 319-20.
50. *Ibid.* p.159.
51. *Ibid.* p.181.
52. *Ibid.* pp. 205-228.
53. *Ibid.* pp. 231-248.

PART – II

APPROACHES TO HISTORY

4

NATURE AND INTERPRETATION OF HISTORY

History is as important as the man himself. Since man discovered the art of writing it is conveyed apart from some other forms, in writing from one generation to another generation. In different space and time its format has been changing, so has been its interpretation. It is called the memory of the society and an attempt to search for truth. The truth whether pleasant or unpleasant must be conveyed, that the ideal set for history. We must accept the truth and if the need be issue a corrective rather than denying or concealing the truth. We also know that various kinds of pressures, prejudices or predilections work in our minds when we begin to write history. Not only that every generation writes history for itself. So there is always a revision in history. It addresses new questions in a new way and tries to search for answers in its own manner. The questions and initiatives taken by the old generation become meaningless or go behind the curtain while the new ones surface the audience. The manner and method of recording history also change with time. Apart from the liberal education, the post-modernist approach to history is also more liberal and elastic. It gives room to everyone to write history and is generous enough to accommodate all biases and predilections to write and support an holistic approach to history where all points, views and approaches find room for them. It has widened the scope and task of history. Some elite have started questioning the use of history and its authenticity as it covers a wider spectrum and view-points connected with the event. This should not be taken as its weakness but its strength by which it has survived and will survive the criticism, which is inherent in the nature of history. History will never die out; it goes on facing all criticism from strength to strength. It will survive with the society and move along with the trends in society wearing varying costumes and designs prevalent in the contemporary society which we may call approaches to history, viz., imperial, nationalist, ethiological, communal, regional, local, historiophoty, ideological, scientific, traditional, Marxist, subaltern, annals and ethnographical or Ethno-archaeological, so on and so forth.

We may draw in this context from Edward W. Said who clearly distinguishes between the knowledge about the natural world and the knowledge about society, the latter he calls as historical knowledge, which rests upon judgement and interpretation. "This is not to say that facts or data are non-existent, but the facts get their importance from what is made of them in interpretation. No one disputes the fact that Napoleon actually lived and was a French emperor; there is, however, a great deal of interpretative disagreement as to whether he was a great or in some ways a disastrous ruler of France. Such disagreements are the stuff out of which historical writing is made and from which historical knowledge derives. For interpretations depend very much on who the interpreter is, who he or she is addressing, what his or her purpose is in interpreting, at what historical moment the interpretation takes place. In this sense, interpretations are what might be called *situational*: they always occur in a situation whose bearing on the interpretation is *affiliative*. It is related to what other interpreters have said, either by confirming them, or by disputing them or by continuing them. No interpretation is without precedents or without some connection to other interpretations ... No writing is (or can be) so new as to be completely original, for in writing about human society, one is not doing mathematics, and therefore one cannot aspire to the radical originality possible in that activity."[1]

Thus in human sciences, in spite of following a scientific method and approach, total objectivity is not possible. We may take any account on face value and allow the reader the right to take it as he understands by reading the account. However, we cannot deny that some truth may come out by itself for us when we see both the sides of the coin.

We may consider the following approaches very crucial to the understanding of history:

1. Imperialist approach to history
2. Nationalist approach to history
3. Ethiological approach to history
4. Ethnological and Ethno-archaeological approach to history
5. Socio-economic approach to history
6. Psychological approach to history
7. Ideological approach to history
8. Traditionalist approach to history
9. Marxist approach to history
10. Post-modern approach to history
11. Historiophoty approach to history
12. Communal approach to history
13. Subaltern approach to history
14. The Annales school
15. Mentalities and Michel Foucault's new kind of history
16. Oral approach to history
17. Evolutionary approach to history

It may be stated that some of these approaches are in some way or other overlapping or partly covering the other approach to history and are not truly independent of each other. For example, the ideological approach covers the traditionalist as well as the Marxist approach to history. It may also cover the party dictatorship as had been in Russia or in India Communist/Congress *versus* VHP/BJP approach to history. This has created a stir among the masses over the Ramajanmabhumi *versus* Babri Masjid dispute more voluminously during the last decade and now over the books and syllabi concerning National Council of Educational Research and Training (NCERT) for revision and change of earlier books prescribed for the schools in the country. Actually uproar by both the sides seems to be unnecessary as revisiting history is within the framework of history – in the light of criticism only truth should prevail.

So also can be said about nationalist, regional or local approach to history which is written to highlight the national, regional or local issues or preservation of heritage which covers the ethiological approach as well. Similarly we may talk of the manuals of the districts written by the British collectors in their districts before they were printed as the district Gazetteers that gave local information about the local history, census, categories of population, castes and professions, and ownership of land, yield income and taxation, etc.

REFERENCE

1. Vintage, London, USA, 1981, 1997, pp. 162-163.

5

DEVELOPMENTS IN HISTORIOGRAPHY DURING THE NINETEENTH AND TWENTIETH CENTURIES

"Nothing is more characteristic of the history of the last two hundred years than the demand from within the profession that history must once again become broader, more inclusive, more concerned with the deeper aspects of human experience. There are abundant signs at the end of this post-war decade that we are on the threshold of another period of reconsidering the purposes and methods of history."[1] Historian must accept his responsibility to society, without violating his responsibility to the past though the writing of history must always be changing and varying. History varies as the life and spirit of different ages vary, and that is why at different times and in different countries diverse type of history have prevailed. To the cultural differences must be added the human factor, the obvious individual differences among historians. These differences are decisive in determining the writing of history, even after the discipline of history has been firmly established and even after it has made its uniform demands on historians.

In the nineteenth century, from Niebur's work in 1811 to Bury's lecture in 1903, history came into its own as an independent field of enquiry. It served or tried to serve, its ties with philosophy and literature, seeking to reconstruct the past *wie es eigenlich gewesen*, "as it actually was". Ranke meant this now if history could in fact achieve this kind of exactitude. Historians gained access to government papers. Historians eagerly exploited these archival sources to write history.[2]

Historiography in Germany in the Nineteenth Century (Ranke)

While the school of romantic nationalism was still in the ascendant, a new spirit was introduced into the theory and practice of history. Born in 1795, Ranke was more interested in the past than the present. At Leipsic he enjoyed the lectures of Gotfried Hermann on the Greek poets, but devoted most of his attention to the ancient historians, above all Thucydides. Niebur, he afterwards declared, convinced him that historians could exist in the modern world. He found time for a little philosophy, reading Kant with interest and Fichte with admiration. Ranke was turned to history not by current events, like Niebur and the patriotic school, but by his professional duties. He loved to lecture on Livy and Herodotus, read Niebur again with increased admiration and welcomed Bock's picture of the Athenian state. He gradually extended his vision beyond to the ancient world to the Middle Ages, composing fragments on Carolingian era from the chronicles.

Ranke's first work in 1824 marks the beginning of critical era of historiography; he first applied to modern history the principles of Niebur. Niebur had written several dissertations on the ancient world, which included history of Rome. Neibur achieved for the Roman republic by making it as real and intelligible as a state of the modern world. His second great achievement was the critical examination of the sources and credibility of early Roman history. He approached his enquiry with a feeling of deep responsibility. "In laying down the pen", he wrote, "We must be able to say in the sight of God. I have not knowingly nor without earnest investigation written anything which is not true."[3]

Ranke, in 1824, declared that he had first applied to modern history the principles of Niebur. There was nothing new in his maxims that the nearest witness to the event was the best, and that the letters of the actors were of more value than the anecdotes of the chronicler. Ranke tried to seize the personality of the writer and to enquire whence he derived his information. "Some will copy the ancients, some will seek instruction for the future, some will attack or defend, some will only wish to record facts. Each must be separately studied."[4] He pronounced Guicciardini wholly unworthy of his reputation. "Much of his material was copied from other books, much was false, much was doubtful, speeches were invented, treatises were altered, important facts misrepresented." Ranke admires his fine political instinct, his universal outlook, his freedom from ecclesiastical bias, but he denies him nearly all the virtues of an historian.[5] Ranke never wearied of expressing his debt to Niebur, whose bust occupied the place of honour in his study though he declared in old age that he had not thought of Neibur or anybody else. "My practice arose by a sort of necessity, in its own way."[6]

Ranke visited and worked in various archives of different countries and wrote their histories. G.P. Gooch summarises his services to history as follows:

(1) The first was to divorce the study of the past from the passions of the present, and to relate what actually occurred – *wie es eigentlich gewesen*.

(2) The second service was to establish the necessity of founding historical construction on strictly contemporary sources. He was not the first to use the archives, but the first to use them well. When he began to write, historians of high repute believed memoirs and chronicles to be the best authorities. When he laid down his pen, every scholar with a reputation to make or to lose had learned to content himself with nothing less than the papers and correspondence of the actors themselves and those in immediate contact with the events.

(3) Thirdly, he founded the science of evidence by the analysis of authorities, contemporary or otherwise, in the light of the author's temperament, affiliations and opportunity of knowledge and by comparison with the testimony of other writers. Henceforth every historian must inquire where his informant obtained his facts. It is Ranke's glory to have rendered the history of modern Europe fully intelligible, to have established its unity and portrayed the leading actors in the drama… He was beyond comparison the greatest writer of modern times, not only because he founded the scientific study of materials and possessed in an unrivalled degree the judicial temper, but because his powers of work and length of life enabled him to produce a large number of first-rate works than any other writer. It was he who made German scholarship supreme in Europe; and no

> one has ever approximated so closely to the ideal historian."[7] Ranke also invented seminar method, which was commenced in 1833 and was attended by a group of students, everyone of whom was to win fame in the boundless fields of research.[8]

When Ranke was surrounded by his children and grand-children he used to say, "I have another and older family, my pupils and their pupils."[9] In preface to his first book, *Histories of the Latin and Germanic Nations, 1494-1514* (1824) Ranke wrote: "To history has been assigned the office of judging the past, of instructing the present for the benefit of future ages. To such high offices this work does not aspire: it wants only to show what actually happened (*wie es eigentlich gewesen*).

But Ranke had his critics in such German historians of the nineteenth century as Duhrung, Droysen, Lorenz and Lamprecht. John Gustav Droysen (1808-84), Professor of History at Berlin was responsible for the famous remark that the objectivity of Ranke was "the objectivity of a eunuch."[10]

In the nineteenth century, there were various attempts to counter positivism and establish a 'scientific' history, which could establish general laws akin to natural science, partly indeed as a reaction against those followers of Ranke who repeated by Rote that history could not answer questions, could only show "how things really were". Auguste Comte's (1798-1857) two major works, *Course of Positivist Philosophy* (1830-42) and *System of Positivist Politics* (1851-54), which certainly did not justify the claims he made for his 'positivism'. Much wider claims were made for the theory of history which originated with Karl Marx, born in 1818 in Germany but he lived much of his writing life in England, where he died in 1883. He never presented a full and rounded account of his theory, known as the Marxist or the 'materialist' interpretation of history. The fullest early statement of this interpretation appeared in the *German Ideology*, written in collaboration with Friedrich Engels and completed in 1846, though only a part was published during Marx's lifetime, no complete edition appeared till 1932. The Communist Manifesto appeared in 1848, in which Engels again collaborated and a brief summary in the Preface (first published posthumously in 1897) which Marx wrote for his *A Contribution to the Critique of Political Economy* (first published in 1859). His major work, *Capital* (1867-94) concentrates on the development of the capitalist economy, which Marx saw the dynamic factor in modern history. Other writings by Marx and by his close associate Friedrich Engels; add various glosses, to this have been added the explanations and extrapolations of admirers and disciples, both scholarly and polemical.[11] "If much tedious rubbish has been written by Marxist historians (leaving aside the propagandist official histories of allegedly 'Marxist countries', it must also be said that some of the most stimulating of all historical work being written today is that of the scholars who are happy and proud to describe themselves as 'Marxists'... To talk of a Marxist school of history is probably to exaggerate Marx's influence as a historian, but it is impossible to deny his influence in some manner or another on almost everything of importance relating to history"[12] published since the nineteenth century... Modern historians do not usually approve grand theories of historical development as they lack the quality of understanding the past from the inside, which is at the base of all true historical study. Perhaps there was some room for essential interconnections after too literal interpretation of the Rankean teachings, which laid too great a stress on mere accumulation of facts, which the positivists and the Marxists tried to make up. Thomas Henry Buckle (1821-62) tried to follow the positivists in search for general laws of human development in his *History of Civilization in England* (the two volumes published in 1856 and 1861 which covered European as well as English history), which according to Marwick 'has led to results very prejudicial to the progress of our knowledge.'[13]

The Berlin revolution in historical studies slowly affected history in Britain and America. In Britain Rankean influence was to develop history as a literary art than as a science.

REFERENCES

1. Fritz Stern, *The Varieties of History*, The World Publishing Company, 1996, 1970, Introduction, p.12.
2. *Ibid.* pp. 13-19.

3. G.P. Gooch, *History and Historians in the Nineteenth Century*, Longmans Green and Co. London, 1920, p.19.
4. *Ibid.* p.79.
5. *Ibid.*
6. *Ibid.*
7. *Ibid.* p.102.
8. *Ibid.* p.113.
9. *Ibid.* p.117.
10. Arthur Marwick, *The Nature of History*, The Macmillan Press, London, 1970, p.38.
11. *Ibid.* p.41.
12. *Ibid.* pp. 41-42.
13. *Ibid.* p.43.

6

TWENTIETH CENTURY HISTORIOGRAPHY

History emphasized on what has been than what now is. However in the twentieth century it has been stated that history should utilize the methods and insights of other social sciences. The very diversity of human experience was a source of strength for the *French Annales School*. In the years around the Second World War Marxist history laid its focus on economic determinism, which was followed by social history, which during the last two decades has been replete with qualitative method and quantification of data. Group research has taken the place of an individual scholar and the role of history is being questioned due to extensive model building of the social science historians.[1] Richard J. Evans of the University of Cambridge reviews the book of George G. Iggers on *New Directions in European Historiography* (1975) and the extensively revised book in English in 1997 recounting the revolution brought about by Leopold Von Ranke in the middle of the nineteenth century. It emphasized on rigour of source–criticism and the use of original documents as the basis for a properly scientific and objective appropriation of the past. From the 1870s historical studies underwent professionalization. Historians made use of archival evidence to support their nationalistic and class preconceptions and gave them the aura of scientific authority, which brought about a 'crisis of classical historicism' due to abundant contradictions, which became obvious by the end of nineteenth century.[2] These new developments in the rise of *French Annales School*, the emergence of a neo-Weberian form of social history in Germany and the rise of the British Marxist historians, all of these emphasized the rigorous use of quantification and social science theory in the search for a new degree of objectivity which actually caused a confusion in the social-scientific approach to history. This gave way to culture, which became the key-organizing concept for the historian. About the criticism of the post-modernists, history strictly represents social reality otherwise we should stop writing history and reading history which is more at the beginning of the twenty-first century than at any time during the previous hundred years. Iggers is clear enough about the role of the historian in capitalist society, his function in the age of nationalism in the nineteenth century. He further comments "If student enrollments in history have fallen in recent years, then this seems to have been compensated for by the current boom in popularity experienced by history on television, radio, the cinema, novels and above all in history books themselves, which are now selling better to the general readership than they have done for many a year. Even the material base of history in Germany differs from that of Britain, is producing different kinds of historical work in the two countries. Richard J. Evans seriously questions Iggers What principle of selection is he adopting? "Tens of thousands of historians have practiced their profession in the twentieth century, only a handful are represented here. An important school of post-colonial historiography such as the subaltern studies group in India receives no mention at all. Braudel's *Mediterranean* or Thompson's *Making of the English Working Class* have been cited more than most... Military history also accounts for a very substantial proportion of publications, as does biography... Similarly the linguistic approach adopted by Joan Scott on the rise of feminist history as one of the major developments of the late twentieth century has been discussed."[3]

REFERENCES

1. Adam Kuper and Jessica Kuper, *The Social Science Encyclopaedia*, London 1985, pp.358-361.
2. *History and Theory* 41 (February 2002) p.79.
3. *Ibid.* pp. 80-85.

7

ETHOLOGICAL OR SOCIO-BIOLOGICAL VIEW OF HISTORY

If we turn the pages of history, right down to our own time, the fate of nations has depended on the outcome of battles, and in history books, wars mark, like milestones, the development of mankind.[1] Since ethology is the study of the biology of behaviour, and has developed out of biology, it has introduced the methods and approaches of biology into the study of behaviour. Like all the other behaviour sciences, ethology looks for the causes of behaviour. But in inquiring why an animal behaves in a specific manner, we ethologists do not limit ourselves to studying the causative physiological mechanisms, the releasing stimuli and the processes of individual development; we approach the question from the point of view of selection (what purpose does this behaviour serve?), and associated with that we also enquire into its polygenetic and historical development.[2]

There is also the other side of the coin that man hopes for and aspires to world peace. Of all the species that have maintained themselves as agents of the stream of life, ours is the only one characterized by a new evolutionary principle, which we describe as cultural evolution. In cultural evolution knowledge is similarly accumulated, not in the genotype but in the brain; since the development of writing, it has also been accumulated in books, and in recent times, in electronic apparatuses as well.[3] Man in India may think he is God's creation; inherently biological factors play a key role in life man as biological creation and he thinks everything in context of their kinship, territory and inheritance of profession or livelihood. Man should show rationalistic behaviour but in many decisions taken by him he behaves instinctively, i.e. to satisfy what serves his instinct personally or socially. Instinct is more important than reason because of biological factors. The decisions are made on votes than on rationale. This leads to a tribal morality, which allows no say to outsiders who may say that neither, we have the soil nor the crowd, as we are outsiders. Spencer and Darwin call for survival of the fittest. For the 'fittest' the definition in 21st century has changed from physical to culture that as a person who has the knowledge and power of pen dominates. Now knowledge is interpreted in the form of superior technology. Now everything is done under the name of culture. Slowly biological behaviour has merged into culture. The conflicts in North-Eastern India, Kashmir problem between India and Pakistan, the protracted and prolonged struggle between Palestine and Israel, the blowing up of World Trade Tower in New York in September 11, 2001 are cases in point. Though we talk of peaceful co-existence still these conflicts go on and see no end to themselves.

Anthropological Approach

Anthropologists emphasise the study of society through field-work, go to the village, live among the tribes, some of them are still living in the age-old traditions and customs, familiarize yourself with them and study them closely. This may be termed simply as ethnological approach. The anthropologist studies them and reports as he sees them and finds them. He notices some variations in the custom and traditions and reports them as it is. For example, *jajmani* system has been functioning in village India since centuries. Anthropological discourses on this traditional Indian rural institution, usually hover around either a single system immutable model like that of Wiser or Dumont, or the multiple system models of Parry, Raheja, Lerche, and others. It has been suggested that neither of these models satisfactorily explains the nature of inter-*jati* exchange relations in rural India. It is, therefore, imperative to simultaneously examine the basic ideology behind these relations and the impacts of many socio-political and historical forces to derive a locally adaptive form of such basic ideology. It has been found that the *jati* dynamics in its locally adaptive form does not necessarily contradict the basic principles of *jati* organization; similarly, the inter-*jati* exchange relations may take different forms for meeting the common goal of survival needs.[4]

Another aspect related to it is ethno-archaeological approach where anthropological and archeological data are collated and help the analysis of the situation, which may be accepted, modified or changed with the new experience.

REFERENCES

1. Irenans Eibb-Eibesfeldt, *The Biology of Peace and War*, Thames and Hudson, Great Britain, 1979, p.1.
2. *Ibid*. pp. 7-8.
3. *Ibid*. pp. 1, 24.
4. Personal Communication from Prof. Kamal K. Misra, Head, Department of Anthropology, HCU, Hyderabad: His paper on this aspect has been accepted for publication in the *Journal of Indian Anthropological Society*, Calcutta, Vol. 37, No.3 (2002).

8

NATIONALIST APPROACH TO HISTORY

Ranajit Guha in his S.G. Deuskar lectures on Indian History 1987[1] quotes Bankimchandra who said in 1880, "to become a nation, a country must have its own history." The British rulers sought to explore the relation between power and property: who owned the land – the king or the landed classes the best answer is Alexander Dow's well-known work, *The History of Hindustan*, published in three volumes in 1768-72, was one of the best examples of this type. Similarly the work on political economy by Grant and thirdly, the local reports focused on how much share of the produce did the landlord pass on to the state? These narratives taken together form the beginnings of colonialist historiography of India.[2] There was no Indian history written by a British author during the late eighteenth century, which did not show signs of such struggle. The discourse grew up to be in the nineteenth century under the impact of Mill's *History of British India*. Thus an attempt was made to historicise the Indian past. Its purpose was not so much to promote historiography as to enable the East India Company to change its technique for the collection of revenues. That was by new pattern of education by the use of which they exploited middle classes to appropriate for themselves the living past of a colonized people.[3]

On the other hand R.C. Majumdar writes, "The Hindus at the beginning of the nineteenth century had no knowledge of their own history and their early attempts to reconstruct it were not only crude but almost ridiculous. Consequently the first English writers on Indian history possessed very little knowledge of Ancient India, and though they had fairly developed ideas of historiography their accounts of Ancient India were very poor and sometimes even ridiculous. For all practical purposes, therefore, the history of Ancient India, up to the middle of the nineteenth century, was treated in a very summary way and mainly as a background of the history of the Muhammadan and British periods."[4]

No Indian historian dared reveal the whole truth when it was likely to offend the government, and that accounts for the virtual absence of true history of the British period written by any Indian. Even the British D. Cunningham, the author of *History of the Sikhs* (Calcutta, 1904) which first appeared in 1849 was severely dealt with which the Governor General of the day, the Marquis of Dalhousie rendered the publication of it a crime, removed Cunningham from his job due to which he died of a broken heart.[5]

The interpretation of Indian history from the eighteenth century onwards has been projected from European point of view, in particular by the British historians who provided initial historiographical base. James Mill wrote with a great prejudice against the Hindus, both on racial and political grounds totally ignoring the facts stated by Orientalists like Sir William Jones. Similarly in V.A. Smith's work *Early History of India* though published a century later and claimed to be written on the basis of latest researches and archaeological explorations we hear the voice of a British member of the Indian Civil Service Smith projects Alexander as a European and Puru as a representative of Asiatic Army. "The triumphant progress of Alexander from the Himalayas to the sea demonstrated the inherent weakness of the greatest Asiatic armies when confronted with European skill and discipline."[6] Similarly Smith describes the post-Harshvardhana period as "the bewildering annals of Indian petty states when left to their own devices for several centuries."[7] History became a means for propagating their interests. The theory of the Aryan race was created on the basis of the word *Arya* that occurs in both the Iranian Avestan and Vedic Sanskrit texts, was given a racial connotation, describing it as a branch of the Indo-European race, which conquered the indigenous people in the second millennium B.C. and established the Vedic Aryan culture.[8] As a result an Aryan and Dravidian dichotomy was created among Indians.

With the publication of James Mill's *History of British India* in early 19th century the Utilitarianism of Mill recommended a radical alteration of Indian society by imposing the correct legal and administrative system in India. Also implicit in Mill's history, was the theory of *Oriental Despotism*, the central question, on the analogy of France and England, was seen as that of private property in land and the state ownership of land. It was maintained that there was an absence of the right to private property in land, which became a model of social and economic structure. The king was seen at the apex, and self-sufficient, isolated village communities at the base. The surplus was collected from the cultivators by the bureaucracy and the process of redistribution led to being appropriated, substantially, by the king and court and hence the fabulous wealth of oriental courts.

Nationalist historical writing took up the theme, among other things, of the importance of religion to Indian society.[9] Indian historians wrote with national sentiments and patriotic fervour, which magnified the virtues and minimized the defects of their own people. It was partly a reactionary writing against the undue depreciation of the Indians in the pages of British histories like those of Mill, and partly an effect of the growth of national consciousness and a desire for improvement in their political status. These defects gained momentum with the movement for political reforms, which was followed up during the freedom movement. For example, K.P. Jayaswal voiced the existence of republican and oligarchical forms of Government in his *Hindu Polity* and asserted for his theory of a Parliamentary form of government in Ancient India against the repeated declarations of British historians that absolute despotism was the only form of government in Ancient India.[10] As regards Medieval India, a conscious attempt was made to rewrite the whole chapter of the bigotry and intolerance of the Muslim rulers towards Hindu religion.[11] Majumdar states that this was prompted by the political motive of bringing together the Hindus and Muslims in a common fight against the British. Another example he quotes a history written under the auspices of the Indian National Congress sought to repudiate the charge that the Muslim rulers ever broke any Hindu temple and asserted that they were the most tolerant in matters of religion. Further he quotes the examples of exonerating Mahmud of Ghazni's bigotry and fanaticism as well as the charge of breaking Hindu temples brought against Aurangzeb terming it as a disputed point.

Similarly late K.M. Ashraf sought to prove that the Hindus and Muslims had no cultural conflict. Similar is the assertion by Lala Lajpat Rai that "the Muslim rule in India was not a foreign rule".[12]

Majumdar states further: "coming to the British period, national sentiments prejudiced a calm consideration of several episodes. Two of them are :

(1) The Black Hole tragedy and character of Siraju-daulah; and
(2) The nature of the outbreak of 1857.

The historians have been influenced by racial or national sentiments. Similarly, many questions concerning economic and administrative systems in almost all of which the British and Indian views have been influenced more or less by national or patriotic feelings."[13]

REFERENCES

1. Ranajit Guha, *An Indian Historiography of India*, Calcutta, 1988, p.1.
2. *Ibid.* p.9.
3. *Ibid.* pp. 17-18.
4. R.C. Majumdar, *Historiography in Modern India*, Bombay, 1970, pp. 5-6.
5. *Ibid.* p.47.
6. *Ibid.* p. 42.
7. *Ibid.* p.41.
8. Romila Thapar, *Interpreting Early India*, OUP, Delhi, 1997 edition, p.3.
9. *Ibid.* p.7.
10. R.C. Majumdhar, *op.cit.*, pp. 47-48.
11. *Ibid.* p.48.
12. *Ibid.* pp. 48-49.
13. *Ibid.* p.49.

9

MARXISM AND HISTORICAL WRITING

"Karl Marx (1813-1883) and Friedrich Engels (1820-1895) are not usually remembered as historians – the standard works on historiography barely mention them – and yet they were not only practicing historians but their *dialectical materialistic conception of history* was the core of their system and made a profound impact on subsequent historical thought and writing. For Marx himself the formulation of historical materialism in the mid-1840s represented the link between his earlier philosophical interest and his later concern with the economic structure and the political development of capitalistic society."[1] His first exposition of his historical materialism in 1932, he said: "Life is not determined by consciousness, but consciousness by life". The modes of production and the social relations to which they give rise determine the consciousness of men, the ideological superstructure of society."[2] The *Communist Manifesto*, published at the end of February 1948 said: "The history of all hitherto existing society is the history of the class struggle Freeman and slave, patrician and plebian, lord and serf, guild-master and journeyman, in a word, oppressor and oppressed, stood in constant opposition to one another, carried on an uninterrupted, now hidden, now open fight, a fight that each time ended, either in a revolutionary re-constitution of society at large, or in the common ruin of the contending classes."[3] Marx defined both class and state as a relationship between exploiters and exploited, so once the source of exploitation, private ownership was removed, class and state will lose all validity.[4]

To prove:

(1) That the existence of classes is only bound up with particular, historic phases in the development of production.[5]

(2) That the class-struggle necessarily leads to the dictatorship of the proletariat.
(3) That this dictatorship itself only constitutes the transition to the abolition of all classes and to classless society.[6]

Marx's use of the word 'prove' seems excessive and indeed, many of his predictions turned out to be false – Marx's belief that the revolution would occur in an advanced society like Britain or the United States was never realized. When so-called Marxist revolutions took place, they occurred in largely peasant societies like Russia, China, Cuba or Yugoslavia, and the scenario was very different from that envisaged by Marx. His assumption that free trade would spread throughout the world also proved false, as did his belief that it would assist the cause of internationalism, which would prove stronger than nationalism.[7] In many ways, the last thirty years of his life were a long anti-climax. Domestic problems, financial stringency and increasing illness often made his life a misery.[8] The way Marxists have interpreted his teachings, the Marxist themselves have erred when they extract a rigid determinism from a body of writings so rich in nuances. They also betray Marx when they use this method to take a short-cut though the complexities of history.[9]

In this context Irfan Habib has stated that it is inherent in the unity of past and present that Marxist historiography must continuously turn to fresh aspects to explore or re-explore and fresh questions to answer. Nothing is more illustrative of this need than the history of Socialist societies, since 1917... Naturally, this can be done on the basis of research and extended knowledge. It has to be an increasing process. There are rival interpretations arising all the time.[10] While Alvin W. Gouldner talks of *The Two Marxisms*: one conceiving Marxism as "critique" and the other social "science". Thus there has been a division between critical Marxists and Scientific Marxists. Marxism intervenes to change the world.[11] "Marx was a paradoxically idealistic materialist who suppressed his own idealism, declaring that he was not really pursuing an ideal but (like Socrates) was only a mid-wife delivering what had been prepared in the womb of history, and calling upon others to do likewise. This ambiguity is reproduced in his conception of "praxis".[12] In one part Marxism is a philosophy of praxis, in another it is a "science", i.e., the political economy of the laws of capitalism.

G.A. Cohen who came in defence of Marxism states "Marx was a restless and creative thinker, who developed many ideas in many directions. He did not have the time or the will, or the academic peace, to straighten them all out. It is not arrogant to claim to offer a less untidy version of some of his major thoughts than he himself provided."[13] Cohen further states, "For it is an old-fashioned historical materialism which I defend, a traditional conception, in which history is, fundamentally, the growth of human productive power, and forms of society rise and fall according as they enable or impede that growth. The focus is on the more basic concepts of the theory, those of forces and relations of production, and there will be unusually little dissuasion, as books on Marx and society go, of class conflict, ideology, and the state."[14] While Paul Q. Hirst criticises Cohen stating that "Marx's theory is more faithful to Hegel than Cohen's, for if humanity is the subject of history its development proceeds through the contradictory movement of a series of social totalities. Mode of production for Marx is a totality and not an assemblage of externally related parts."[15] He ridicules Cohen's thesis as an illusion.

Georg G. Iggers points out to a sharp contrast in relation of Marxist economists and Marxist historians. The Marxists did not succeed in linking their strict models of economic development with the analysis of historical events, except by means of broad generalizations incapable of empirical validation.[16]

However Mayer has written in defence of Analytical Marxism according to him Marxism project should be understood as the effort to create a scientific theory of the practice of human emancipation from economic domination.[17]

REFERENCES

1. Fritz Stern, *The Varieties of History*, New York, second edition, 1970; p.145.
2. *Ibid.*

3. "John Whittam, Karl Marx" in John Cannon (ed.) *The Historian at Work*, p.97.
4. *Ibid.*
5. R.H. Tawney, *Religion and the Rise of Capitalism*, Pelican England, 1922, Reprinted 1980.
6. *Ibid.* p.98
7. *Ibid.*
8. *Ibid.* p.99.
9. *Ibid.* p. 101.
10. Irfan Habib, "Problems of Marxist Historiography" in *Social Scientist*, Vol. 16, Number 12, December 1988, p.3.
11. Alvin W. Gouldner, *The Two Marxisms*, London, 1980, p.32.
12. *Ibid.* p.33.
13. G.A. Cohen, *Karl Marx's Theory of History: A Defence*, Oxford, 1978, see Foreword, p.IX.
14. *Ibid.* p. X.
15. Paul Q. Hirst, *Marxism and Historical Writing*, London, 1985, p.31.
16. Georg G. Iggers, *New Dimensions in European Historiography*, Methuen, 1985, pp. 123-124.
17. Thomas F. Mayer, "In Defence of Analytical Marxism", in *Science and Society*, Vol. 53, No.4, Winter, 1989, pp. 416-441.

10

SUBALTERN HISTORIOGRAPHY

Ranajit Guha and his historian colleagues in India and abroad have enunciated an important approach to the study of tribal/peasant movements. Designated as 'subaltern' historiography, this approach seeks to restore a balance by highlighting the role of the politics of the people as against elite politics played in Indian history. Thus 'elite' and 'people' are viewed as binary domains to constitute a structural dichotomy.[1] It claims to be an improvement on the elitist mode (both Marxist and Non-Marxist type) of exploring and explaining history. We may call it 'history from below'.[2] It is society's own expression about itself. It is collected and recollected history recorded from the memory and lips of informants.[3] The practitioners of this subaltern model like Shahid Amin, Partha Chatterjee, David Hardiman, Gyanendra Pandey, Ramachandra Guha, Tanika Sarkar, Sumit Sarkar and Kapil Kumar have contributed to the subaltern studies series initiated by Ranajit Guha. Shahid states that there was no single authorized version of Mahatma Gandhi to which peasants of eastern U.P. and north Bihar may be said to have subscribed in 1921.[4] Some scholars like Sumit Sarkar are criticising the statements for what they were rallying around the subaltern. Hence Christopher Hill while reviewing Vol. IX of the *Subaltern Studies* which is related to writing on South Asian History and Society has narrated a joke. Reader to the Author: "I cannot understand what you are saying". Author: "Too bad. The problem is that you are unsophisticated and untrained reader. If you were smarter, you would understand me." "The fact that the founding fathers of subaltern studies, whose works in general provide superb examples of rigorous local research, were nonetheless unsure of exactly how they had changed the face of peasant studies. Surely some of the non-subaltern work deserves to be recognized."[5]

The subaltern studies suffer from the same contradiction, which they levelled against the elite for writing self-history by self. It has been stated that there were two sets of exploiters: a reactionary elite, composed of landlords and external colonizers and a progressive one, in which rich proprietors led peasants against planters and landlords.[6] Sarkar has now joined not only oppositional discourse of subaltern studies but has learned to emphasize on cultural difference and on the other the right wing/ conservative Third World nationalism of the BJP/VHP/RSS.[7] The kind of Marxism Sarkar now defends, the 'from-below' historiography of E.P. Thompson, is in many important respects no different from the post-modern 'new' populism informing the subaltern studies project.[8] However, adherents to the subaltern historiography emphasise that the neo-nationalist variety has always over-stated the part elite has played in building Indian nationalism but has failed to recognize the contribution made by people (masses) on their own, independently of the elite. Subaltern historiography treats people (subalternity) as an autonomous domain that originates neither from elite politics nor depends on them. Guha also clarifies that the two domains have not been sealed off from each other but often overlapped.

Guha accepts that his approach to the study of social movements basically forms a part of the general tradition of scientific Marxism though deduced from A. Gramsci's formulations. He hints out at the conventional discourses on peasant/tribal insurgencies, which hitherto have served in the colonialist historiography as merely an apology for law and order.[9] The peasant and tribal tenantory rebelled against *Sarkari*, *Sahukari*, and *Zamindari* oppression to which they were subjected. The uprisings of Bhumji, the Kol insurrection, the Santal revolt of 1855, the Indigo disturbances of 1859-62 and the Deccan riots of 1875 in the nineteenth century or the left-wing insurrectionary struggles of peasants (such as the Tebhaga or Telangana struggles) of the twentieth century in India come to mind almost immediately. However, Guha states that the twentieth century movements of the peasantry and tribals have been qualitatively different and decisively *more advanced*, which refer to level of conciousness, organization and ideological articulation. From the study of various tribal movements of 1793-1900 period, Guha has constructed six paradigmatic forms – negation, ambiguity, modality, solidarity, transmission and territoriality.[10]

Negation

(1) Taking a cue from Gramsci again, Guha regards negativity as the first glimmer of that consciousness. Accompanied by the ability to discriminate friends from foes, negation often results in selective violence only against the perceived enemies.

(2) The second form 'ambiguity' draws the basic difference between 'crime' and 'insurgency'. Crime tends to be an individualistic or small group-oriented, but secretive or conspiratorial action. In contrast, insurgency has a mass character, which manifests publicly.

(3) '*Modality*' – the next (third) elementary aspect – is a logical extension of the public character of tribal or peasant insurgencies. It is often formalized by the general body of insurgents through ritual presentation of *nazranas*, which marks validation, and sacrilisation of rebel violence as a public service.[11]

(4) '*Solidarity*' – signifies separation of his own identity from that of his enemies which means 'collective consciousness' or class solidarity. The solidarity of the rebel peasant or tribal manifests in chastisement of traitors.

(5) '*Transmission*' as a form/aspect of peasant or tribal insurgency, Guha deals with the patterns of spread of insurgency.

(6) Lastly, '*territoriality*' is that aspect or form of peasant/tribal consciousness in which insurgents get bound by blood ties (consanguinity) on the one hand and by local bond (contiguity) on the other.

The subaltern approach as it developed in India represents a synthesis of four major streams within contemporary Marxism:

(1) *Gramscian Marxism*: which emphasizes the role of pure spontaneity of the action of subaltern masses in history in general and under a hegemonic state in particular;

(2) *Trotskyite Marxism*: particularly in terms of consciousness, considers the role of party, strategies and tactics as important, no doubt, but not as prior to 'necessary consciousness';

(3) The third Marxist stream which Guha's own approach draws inspiration from is represented by Eric

Hobsbawm, George Rude and E.P. Thompson, who through their studies have shown the indispensability of the material force and actors of history; and

(4) In terms of the directions in which subaltern struggles develop, or the forms in which they manifest, Guha and his associates have the model in 1968 Paris Uprising (i.e. the massive student and youth protest) that finally, brought the downfall of Charles de Gaulle, the Latin American movements – particularly the experience of Che Guevera in Bolivia and the like. It is a blend of these four traditions in contemporary Marxism that Guha's subaltern studies approach to history represents. Dhanagare also accepts that the 'Subaltern Studies' earned its friends and critics both, particularly young historians as followers who have focused their attention on peasants, workers and other subaltern elements. Critics of the 'Subaltern Studies' approach have attacked precisely the whole notion of 'autonomy' of the subaltern consciousness. Secondly, the composition of this category is not homogeneous. More importantly, the Subaltern Studies approach to historiography mostly confines to the colonial period, though not all adherents strictly do so.[12] All the studies on agricultural labourers or jute workers do not fit into the 'subaltern studies' straitjacket, e.g. David Hardiman's study on the *devi* movement among the tribals of Gujarat. Though mainly 'insurgencies' should form the part of movement but subaltern series have dealt with movements – protests/mobilizations, which are not insurgent in character. The peasant movements after 1950s, which gathered momentum since the phase of planned rural development, did not develop necessarily along the insurgent syndrome. The identity formations of ethnic/ tribal groups, peasantry, or even among minorities and their political expressions in contemporary India present a wide spectrum. They range from the nativist movements like the Shiva Sena in Maharashtra (which is militant but not radical), or the movements for assertion of regional/sub-regional identities such as for a separate Vidharba or Telangana state on the one hand and many other 'sons of the soil' movements which have sometimes taken on insurgent, militant, or even terrorist forms but mostly

pursued their demands within the constitutional framework of India. The ideologues of these movements, with the coming of the green revolution and the rise of agricultural production have questioned the profitability due to non-remunerative prices. Ernesto Laclau terms such movements as 'populist movements' whether farmers, ethnic, tribal or regional.[13] As regards an interpretation of populism Laclau terms it as a typical expression of a determinate social class and hence it is both a movement and an ideology at the same time, it may be called theoretical nihilism yet it is difficult to specify common crucial attributes that are present in all movements that are usually characterized as 'populist' though populism has gained more and more respectability in the social sciences. As an ideology it incorporates ingrained hostility of the *status quo* and mistrust of traditional politicians, its appeal to masses and finally, its anti-intellectualism. Dhanagare further goes into the intricacies of 'populism' for which he advocates that Guha's framework of the six forms of rebel's consciousness, and Laclau's formulations on 'populism' could provide us with some directions for further enquiry.[14]

REFERENCES

1. D.N. Dhanagare "Subaltern Consciousness and Populism: Two Approaches in the Study of Social Movements in India", *Social Scientist*, Vol. 16, No.11, November 1988, p.10.
2. I.D. Gaur, "Subaltern Historiography" in S.K. Bajaj, *Recent Trends in Historiography*, p.129.
3. *Ibid.* pp. 137-139.
4. *Ibid.* p.141.
5. Christopher, Hill. *The Journal of Asian Studies*, Vol. 59, No. I, Feb. 2000, pp. 197-198.
6. Tom Brass, "Unmasking the Subaltern or Salamis without Themistocles" in *The Journal of Peasant Studies*, Vol. 28, No.I, October 2000, p.163.
7. *Ibid.* p.161.
8. *Ibid.* p.167.
9. Dhanagare, *op.cit.* p. 21.
10. *Ibid.* p.22.
11. *Ibid.* p.23.
12. *Ibid.* pp. 26-27.
13. *Ibid.* p.29; f.n. 64., Ernesto Laclau, Politics and Ideology in Marxist Theory, London, 1979.
14. *Ibid.* p.33.

11

WOMEN'S HISTORY

In the beginning of the twentieth century, women's history caught attention. Once in England, the women came out of kitchen to help the soldiers in the First World War they never went back to kitchen. First they got was women franchise. Recently women's movement is gaining momentum on the following fronts:

(1) Gender discrimination, socially and economically
(2) Patriarchy
(3) Child labour especially girl child, infanticide
(4) Women education
(5) Women dowry deaths
(6) Women writing in India
(7) Women sexuality
(8) Women empowerment

It was often felt that in India society being patriarchal, everything is talked or written from male point of view and the women are more or less ignored. Hence let them write history from women's point of view.

Geraldine Forbes, author of the *New Cambridge History of India* entitled *Women in Modern India*, New Delhi, 1988 traces their recent history from the nineteenth century under colonial rule, to the twentieth century after independence. In the 1970s the United Nations focused world attention on the status of women and declared 1975-85 Women's decade. Sparrow (Sound and Picture archives for Research on Women) in Bombay is a recent and heroic attempts to preserve Women's documents, especially photographs, films and recordings.[1] The present work is largely based on women's own accounts, which the author had the privilege to go through personally.[2]

The author begins with the reform movement and discusses the role of education in changing their lives enabling them to take part in public life. She documents the formation of their organization, their participation in the struggle for freedom, their role in colonial economy and the development of Women's movement in India since 1947. Susie Tharu and K. Lalita, Tanika Sarkar and Vina Majumdar have actively worked in this direction.[3] Another primary and earlier work on women has been by Dr. A.S. Altekar, *The Position of Women in Hindu Civilization*, which covers the study of women from prehistoric times to the present day.[4] However certain key issues in sociological theory have been raised by Ruth A. Wallace (ed.) in the work *Feminism and Sociological Theory*, London, 1989, such as follows:

Part I covers following issues :

(1) The Dissemination of Feminist Thought: 1960-1988,
(2) Sociological Theory: Methods of Writing Patriarchy,
(3) Making Gender Visible, and
(4) Psychoanalytic Feminism: Implications for sociological theory.

Part II covers a Critique and Revaluation of Existing Theories while Part III takes care of Emerging Feminist Theories.

Finally it indicates a growing interest in theory among women sociologists in the United States.[5]

REFERENCES

1. G. Forbes, *op.cit.*, p.5.
2. *Ibid.* pp. 7-8.
3. *Ibid.* p.11.
4. Delhi, 1938 Reprinted 1973.
5. Ruth A.Wallace (ed.) *Feminism and Sociological Theory*, London, 1989, p.7.

12

THE ANNALES TRADITION
French School of Historians

It has been realized that history reflects the social, political and institutional context within which history is written and that every history possessed validity only for the age and the culture within which it was written.[1] That human actions are governed by mental and physical laws, which it is the task of the historian to discover as history, deals with living men. Understanding of human behaviour in its concrete manifestations did not exclude but rather necessitated causal explanations.[2] The Annales historians are concerned for each historical setting for the 'total' character and differ sharply from that of the American New Economic historians and in France from Quantitative history.[3] In France a challenge to historicist orientation came from a positivistic tradition in sociology. It was sociologists and the philosophers who first challenged the historicism of the historians. Marc Bloch, one of the friends of the *Annals* maintained that "It is human consciousness which is the last analysis in the subject matter of historical studies and that history always has to deal with the beings who are capable of pursuing conscious goals which the historian has to understand.[4] The historian could understand consciousness only indirectly from written or oral statements and pursued the concrete traces of the past. The written documents served the purpose of secondary sources as they reflected the events only through the subjectivity of the observer. They could be viewed as primary sources if they exposed the mentality of a society as in case of laws or business papers – they formed a concrete constituent part of the actions of the society. Thus Bloch like Durkheim shifted the emphasis from individual to the collectivity. The actual history of the Annales does not begin in 1929 but with the foundation by Henri Berr in 1900 to which Lucien Febvre and Marc Bloch collaborated in

1907 and in 1912 respectively. Febvre examined the mental tools of the age on the basis of their concepts and syntax.[5]

Bloch emphasized the material framework within which consciousness expresses itself. Bloch tried to construct a social history of agriculture since the Middle Ages, taking into consideration field patterns, cropping systems and farming techniques. He was not primarily concerned with the mighty, wealthy or the cultured but with serfs and peasants. He was interested in the continuity and development of agriculture and of rural life from the Middle Ages to the present.[6] Bloch viewed feudalism differently from conventional military services and also from Marxian point of view of social mode of production. He tried to reconstitute "a total social ambience" and attempted to redefine the concept of feudalism as a form of society.[7] Marc Bloch was shot dead (June 16, 1944) by the Germans during the war; Lucien Fabvre became the sole editor of *Annales* from 1946 to 1956. Fernand Braudel succeeded Fabvre and finished a model of historical explanation.[8] Braudel had called for an empirical and quantitative history which took biological, geographical and even climatic factors into consideration – harvests, epidemics, nutrition, clothing and fashions, means of production, the distribution of commodities and wealth. But consciously missing from his "total history" was an analysis of institutions and mentalities.[9] The *Annales* have remained a forum for international discussion on the methods of historical studies within the framework of human sciences. Some criticism has been levelled against the *Annales* by Marxists as well as by conventional historians. Braudel assumes that in its scientific procedures, historical research remains relatively independent of ideological bias. The *Annales* historians insist on "specific intentions" to be examined within a structural framework, yet they often ignored them in their own analysis.[10] The *Annales* have widened the scope of the historian's interest to all phases of human social life including the biological aspects, the realm of fantasy and myth-building as well as the broadest expressions not only for the "pre-historic" but also recent periods. Thus *Annales* have become a model of scientific history to historians throughout the world. The Mediterranean sea of the sixteenth century was made the determinant factor for the background of human history, which had helped Braudel to see unity of region. Braudel divided his work into three durees which means duration or unit of time[11] and tried to explain the history of man in relation to geography and climatic environment.[12] Thus *Annales* have become a model of scientific history to historians throughout the world.[13]

Recent Tendencies of Historiography in France

In 1989, the approach of the bicentennial commemoration of the revolution of 1789 brought forth a wave of publications. It had some adverse effect though comparing the two revolutions has certainly helped understand the revolutionary process but in dissimilar contexts – may lead to blurring perspectives and a clouding of judgments.[14] There has been a renewal of political history. Historians discovered that evolutions were unpredictable and that events not only modify the course of history, but also reveal hidden tendencies by suddenly bringing them to the surface. The mechanistic and materialistic vision of history brought into focus the religious history and more recently the cultural history being the youngest member of historiography, which includes the history of mentalities. It is a vast domain, which is just beginning to explore aspects such as history of ideas and the growth of scientific knowledge. There has been a rehabilitation of biographies, that is, professional historians are no longer disdainful of writing these. Marginalised communities and others neglected by history, historical research is particularly concentrating on them as a recent trend in historical research. The question of national identity has given incentive to study on immigrants in France. Many studies have been undertaken on the conditions of women as well as their role in family and society. The debate on memory has taken a central place in the studies of historians.[15] Recent works discern a multiplicity of approaches but Foucault, a twentieth century philosopher and historian has questioned the very texture of history, which is based on a disjuncture and discontinuity between different historians and historical events. Diana, Princess of Wales, could be any attractive young woman but her imminent insertion into the British royal family marked her emergence as a celebrity who was both a product of the media and of social and institutional discourses and an active agent in the production of her own identity.[16] In *The Order of Things*, Certeau described as the history of ideas in Western Europe over the last four hundred years, but it was a history that did not find continuity, progress, origins and that things were 'the same'. He called the periods of history as 'epistemes' – that were organized round their specific worldviews. The rise and fall of these epistemes did not show any continuity or progress and thus challenged the theory of natural evolution and that different epistemes appear and disappear suddenly and equally arbitrarily.[17] Foucault does not see a linear and progressive development from the Renaissance to the Modern age.[18]

REFERENCES

1. Georg G. Iggers, *New Dimensions in European Historiography*, Methuen, 1985, pp. 6-7.
2. *Ibid.* pp. 44-45.
3. *Ibid.* p.44.
4. *Ibid.* p.50.
5. *Ibid.* pp. 52-54.
6. *Ibid.* pp. 54-55.
7. *Ibid.* p. 55.
8. S.K. Bajaj, *Recent Trends in Historiography*, New Delhi, 1988, pp. 44-45.
9. Iggers, *op.cit.,* pp. 63-64.
10. *Ibid.* pp. 74-77.
11. Bajaj, *op.cit.,* pp. 48-49.
12. *Ibid.* p.49.
13. Iggers, *op.cit,.* p.79.
14. *Social Science and Humanities in France*, Ministry of Foreign Affairs, p. 14.
15. Tr. p.3.
16. Geoff Danaher, Tony Schirato *et al., Understanding Foucault*, Delhi, 2001, pp. 162-163.
17. *Ibid.* pp. 15-18.
18. *Ibid.* p. 19.

13

PSYCHOANALYSIS AND HISTORY

Psychoanalysis in Britain formed a strong theory but its impact on wider intellectual culture was initially minimal. The position gradually changed in 1970s when the concept became widespread within film theory and literary criticism and many areas of feminist theory debated the work of Freud and later analysts. In USA psychoanalysis in historical writing has made a considerable progress. *American Historical Review* and the *Journal of Interdisciplinary History* have regularly published psycho-historical articles.[1] Due to stronger position of psychoanalysis within American social and cultural life it has a continuing inter-action between psychoanalysis and social sciences in America since 1930. For example, the disciplines of political science, sociology, anthropology and at later date history may be specified, specially Peter Gay's 985 book: *Freud for Historians* can be mentioned along with W.J. Gilmore's 1984 bibliography *Psychohistorical Enquiry*. The focus is usually on individual biographies, on areas of social life (childhood, the family, sexuality) or on extreme situations (such as fascism or witch-hunting)[2]. There is no unanimity of mental processes and unconscious structures, an emphasis rooted in biology and social construction of human motives and behaviour, within history specifically, an additional stress on changes in such construction over time, since it is believed that there is no universal human nature, only some universal forms of mental functioning.[3] An external event may have varied responses by different individuals but an understanding is very valuable as a corrective to the rather mechanical psychology. For example, reading the debates concerning psycho-analytic interpretations of the career of the American President Woodrow Wilson brings out clearly the difficulty of understanding his actions as *simultaneously* moves within a public political world, and responses to inner needs and drives – the common tendency seems to be to assume that one level of explanation excludes the other.[4] The differences between and the inter-action of, causal and interpretative approaches can be clearly seen within forms of biological writing as Freud's own most powerful inclination towards establishing genetic explanations, the primal scene concealed by a screen memory.[5]

Actually psychological explanation and psycho-analysis could be reserved for what is dubbed irrational. Many accounts of political leaders, artists or writers leave it unclear how they could have achieved what they did in the public realm – some of them are an expression of neurotic, narcissistic or psychopathic pattern. Freud's *Group Psychology* and the *Analysis of the Ego* (1921) concentrated on the relationship between a leader and the group led, with the latter becoming dependent on the leader.[6] This resulted in historians having difficulty in employing psychoanalytic concepts to interpret group processes, which involve wider dynamics than face-to-face interaction. Erikson, building on the work of Freud, has concentrated on the politico-religious figures of Luther and Gandhi also giving much attention to Hitler and various revolutionary leaders (often within the Marxist tradition) but still the relationship between the psychology of the individual leader and the role that leader plays in bringing into being and holding together a group of followers.[7] Still the greater difficulty is visible in attempts to study collective group behaviour, viz.,

(1) How to define or delimit the group of a leader?
(2) How to understand the structuring of such a group as a group?
(3) How to specify sub-divisions within the group?
(4) How to understand the relation between the fantasy of the group and its conscious goals?

These psychological inferences must not, finally be construed as a diagnosis of outright pathology.[8] The involvement of psycho-analysis is also seen in oral history as well[9] which leads to 'participant observation', the ethnographic and life-history orientation. We may refer to the following works:

(1) W.I. Thomas, *The Polish Peasant in Europe and America Around 1920.*

(2) *The Child in America (1928).*
(3) *The Unadjusted Girl (1923).*

In addition the Chicago based journal until 1936, *The American Journal of Sociology* carried many psychoanalytic articles.[10]

We also find a notable article by Frank E. Manuel, "The Use and Abuse of Psychology in History".[11] Frank praises Vico, an Italian, a man of the early eighteenth century, to interpret evidence, to recapture the emotions and spirit of the age of heroic barbarism. The great French historian of the nineteenth century, Jules Michelet who translated and commented on the works of Vico showed to the entire world that Vico's dramatization of the Renaissance was a new way of perceiving the world as an innovation in the uses of psychology in history entirely in the spirit of Vico's "New Science" Hegel's contribution to psychological history was passed on to Marx and Kierkegaord and has since been inflated as the central psychological distinction of modern consciousness. In the last decades of the nineteenth century psychology began to achieve its autonomous place in the German academic world. Thus 1880 became a convenient starting point for having a modern relationship of history and psychological.[12] It may be noted that Freud himself and his immediate disciplines came hardly in touch with the academic historians of any country but Dilthey and Febvre represented two different versions of an initial stage in the emergence of psychological history in recent times. Dilthey was of the view that the history of man can best be presented as a series of psychological world outlooks, more significantly emotive than rationalist, embodied mainly in the writings of literary, religious and philosophical geniuses whose expression formed the stuff of history.[13] In theory Dilthey was committed to relating the individual psychological natures of his heroes with the grand world outlooks, which they had evolved.[14] On the other hand Febvre's *Rebelais* is the work in which his particular skill was used in communicating what another epoch, "willed, felt and thought", established *historie psychologique*, its virtues as well as its limitations. While commenting on his subject's religious beliefs, he was able to demonstrate with a plethora of empirical evidence it as anachronism.[15] According to Febvre one of the greatest obstacles in the way of any attempt was to define history of sensibility in a segment of past time. He pleaded for cooperative research between historians and psychologists for which he referred to go to the French psychologists like Dr. Henri Walton. His main objective seemed to capturing the unique sensibility of the past age for a historian, to which all his other efforts were subordinated. Frank further refers to thinkers like Herbert Marcuse and Erik Erikson, leaving aside a large contingent of psychoanalyst who made the United States the world centre of Freudian thought and practice. While Marcuse followed mainly the Marxian-Hegelian worldview, Erikson popularized the term *psycho-history*. Freud himself made a number of applications of psychoanalysis to history. While Freud's historical essays were attacked for errors in detail, his analytic method of gaining access to the unconscious opened a vast new area to historical enquiry.[16] Erikson attempted two studies on Luther and Gandhi and called them politico-religious geniuses, which led to psychological history writing, theorizing that each new generation strives to pass the older one, as in the above two cases, sons had outstripped their fathers and compensated for their failures.[17]

Sartre's existentialist combination of psychology and history, emphasizes the kinds of questions, a historian addresses to his materials. Rereading the histories of the French Revolution, the Revolution of 1848 and the Commune he asks, what really happens when a crowd moves on an objective? What is the nature of the secret psychological commitments and pacts they have made with one another? How in fact does collective historical action came about? In his treatment of individuals Sartre has created prototypes for the fusion of social and psychological knowledge.[18] Lastly, Frank remarks that a certain imperialistic character attaches to a major intellectual discovery such as psychoanalysis. Psychology and history are two different disciplines and combined together they raise more problems than they resolve. He advocates to add a history of other needs and expressions of living.[19]

Finally, we seek to draw attention of the readers to Carl Jung who was the first among modern psychologists to be influenced by Yoga, which enlarged his awareness of his own conscious and provided him with clues as to how to better make present its contents. He refers to mental states (*cittavrtti*) – the psyche. Jung shared this perception of the reality of psychic matter, which is the same as empirical world. In his view the concept of *libido* has functionally the same significance as the concept of energy in physics, which he found endorsed, is *Samkhya-yoga* conception of *Citta*.[20] According to Jung sexuality is an important desire but not the only one. He describes *Klesas* as urges, the natural instinctive forms that represent psychological energy or *libido* in its simplest form of manifestation without which one could never develop an individual personality. For Jung it is the creative individuation of many desires of the collective unconscious that signals a mature and integrated personality.[21]

REFERENCES

1. T.G. Ashplant, "Psychoanalysis in Historical Writing" in *History Workshop* issue 26, Autumn, London, 1988, p.103.
2. *Ibid.* p. 104.
3. *Ibid.* p. 105.
4. *Ibid.* p. 106.
5. *Ibid.*
6. *Ibid.* p.111.
7. *Ibid.* pp. 111-112.
8. *Ibid.* pp. 112-116.
9. Karl Figlio, "Oral History and the Unconscious" in *History Workshop* 26, London, 1988, pp. 120-151.
10. *Ibid.* p.125.
11. Daedalus, *Journal of American Academy of Arts and Sciences*, Vol. 117, No.3, 1988, pp. 199-225.
12. *Ibid.* pp. 201-203.
13. *Ibid.* p. 204.
14. *Ibid.*
15. *Ibid.* pp. 206-207.
16. *Ibid.* pp. 210-211.
17. *Ibid.* pp. 213-214.
18. *Ibid.* p.215.
19. *Ibid.* pp. 216-223.
20. Harold Coward, "Desire in Yoga and Jung", *JICPR* Vol. V, 1987, pp. 57-58.
21. *Ibid.* pp. 60-63.s

14

ORAL HISTORY

All history depends ultimately upon the social purpose it serves. Since the social purpose of history demands an understanding of the past, which relates directly or indirectly to the present, most historians make implicit or explicit judgements – quite properly. Reality is complex and many-sided; and it is a primary merit of oral history that to a much greater extent than most sources it allows the original multiplicity of standpoints to be recreated. Moreover oral history is a history built around people.[1] It thrusts life into history itself and it widens its scope. It allows heroes not just from the leaders, but also from the unknown majority of people. It offers a challenge to the accepted myths of history and provides a means for a radical transformation of the social meaning of history.[2]

In fact oral history is as old as history itself. It was the first kind of history. Since oral tradition itself was very varied, Jan Vasina in his classic *Oral Tradition : A Study in Historical Methodology* (1965), divided African Oral tradition into five categories:

(1) First, there are formulas – learning formulas, rituals, slogans and titles.
(2) Next there are lists of place names and personal names.
(3) Then come official and private poetry – historical, religious or personal.
(4) Fourthly, there are stories – historical, didactic, artistic or personal.
(5) Lastly, there are legal and other commentaries.

Not all of these can be found in all African societies: official poetry and historical stories, for example, arise only with a relatively high degree of political organization. The social importance of some of these oral traditions also resulted in reliable systems for handing them down from generation to generation with a minimum of distortion.[3]

During the nineteenth century came into vogue the fieldwork method, historical analysis and social theory. The most important communications between people are made orally by meeting or telephone, the record is taken as a document for future. The American Oral History Association was established in 1948 when Allan Nevins began recording the memories of persons significant in American life. Very recently the method has been revived to cover up Indian History, black history, folklore and Women's history. The Canadian Oral History Association was formed in 1974.[4] Actually the information provided by oral history should be synthesized with other historical source material.[5] In 1967 Oxford University Press began publishing its *Urban Life in America Series* under the general editorship of Richard C. Wade. In the early 1970s we notice the *Harvard Studies in Urban History*, which stated that until now, the historical character of the urbanization process did not receive the fundamental scholarly research necessary for placing it on solid intellectual foundations.[6] There was convergence of sociology and history. British sociology expanded rapidly in 1960s and at the same time showed an increasing concern with a historical dimension in social sciences. Since then oral history has grown fast in Britain.[7]

Oral history has grown where there was a surviving tradition of fieldwork within history itself, as with political history, labour and local history, or where historians have been brought into contact with other fieldwork disciplines such as sociology, anthropology, or dialect and folklore research. There are even oral history projects on the fund-giving foundations themselves apart from the dominant private funding.[8] Statistical history can no more unravel the past unaided than sociology can provide answers to all current social problems.[9] In economic history and demography we do find supporters of oral history. If the full potential of oral history is realized, it will add a new dimension to history.[10] Oral history is essential to secure reliable information on labour patterns or the variations in technological level. It is all the more required for oral fieldwork in agricultural economic history. So also in the history of religion, oral sources can be utilized to distinguish the beliefs and practices of ordinary adherents from those of their leaders. How far, for example, the religion shaped the values of lower middle class white-collar worker? Since the relationship between economic development and the religious ideologies of entrepreneurs and their workforces has long been a key subject of historical debate, this provides another point where oral evidence can continue economic history.[11] Oral evidence can also be used to amplify information on specific events in labour history, such as evolution of an organization.[12] Oral history can be used for documentation of Women's history which has been largely ignored by historians until very recently partly because their lives so often passed undocumented, tied to the home or to unorganized or temporary work. Similarly we can probe into the social history of a minority group, say blacks to know what is distinctive about them as history?[13] So it can be treated as one more document, which has to be assessed and evaluated in exactly the same way that we evaluate any other kind of historical evidence?[14]

Arthur Marwick in his *The Nature of History* (1970) lists the 'accepted hierarchy' of sources. The most important point is to consider the authenticity of sources of how the document came into being? Who exactly was the author and what was the purpose in writing it.[15]

There is a scope for distortion in the interview situation. Repeat surveys suggest how far any historical or contemporary evidence derived from interviews needs to be treated with care. Both the focus and the texture, of history are changed in a way that only oral evidence could bring about.[16]

Towards the book Paul Thompson points out that oral history is peculiarly suited to project work, which can be taken in many different contexts both as individual and as group enterprises – in schools, colleges, and universities or in adult education group, from museums, or from community centres. For history teachers oral history projects have the special advantages of opening up locally relevant history for exploration. At the University of Essex, where the M.A. in Social History includes a course in the interview method.[17] That the oral history project has its most radical implications, viz., in adult literacy, museum exhibition or a radio programme. Another critical factor in success is the choice of whom to interview. First one should prepare oneself for interview through reading and in other ways, of background information. The best way to start is through exploratory interviews, mapping out a field and picking up ideas and information.[18]

The most recurrent problem is presented by the public personality as informant. After recording has been completed how the tapes should be kept? And how can they be used to make history? We need first to consider the problem of storage and indexing and then the stages in writing and presenting history with oral evidence. Every tape, as soon as used needs to be well labelled.

Lastly, Paul Thompson devises three ways in which oral history can be put together. The first is the single life-story narrative. The second form is a collection of stories. The third form is that of cross-analysis. Argument and cross-analysis are necessary for any systematic development of the interpretation of history.[19]

Adrienne Cooper authored a book on Agrarian Conflicts in Bengal reconstructing with oral evidence.[20] Similarly we quote some other attempts made by the use of oral history in inter-disciplinary direction.[21]

REFERENCES

1. Paul Thompson, *The Voice of the Past Oral History*, OUP, 1978, pp. 1-15.
2. *Ibid.* p.18.
3. *Ibid.* p.20.
4. *Ibid.* pp. 54-55.
5. Bruce M. Stave, *The Making of Urban History*, Historiography Through Oral History, London, 1977, pp. 13-14.
6. *Ibid.* p.15.
7. Paul Thompson, op. cit., p.57.
8. *Ibid.* p.59.
9. *Ibid.* p.61.
10. *Ibid.* pp. 65-66.
11. *Ibid.* pp. 69-70.
12. *Ibid.* p.71.
13. *Ibid.* pp. 87-89.
14. *Ibid.* p.91.
15. *Ibid.*

16. *Ibid.* pp. 119-137.
17. *Ibid.* p.153.
18. *Ibid.* p. 165.
19. *Ibid.* pp. 204-205.
20. Adrienne Cooper, *Sharecropping and Sharecroppers' Struggles in Bengal*, 1930-1950, Calcutta, 1988, pp. 360-*passim*.
21. MLK Murthy and G.D. Sontheimer, "Prehistoric Background to Pastoralism in the Southern Deccan in the light of Oral Traditions and Cults of some Pastoral Communities", *Anthropos*, Vol. 75, 1980;
Satish Saberwal, "Oral Data, Religious Literature and History" in D. Chattopadhyaya (ed.) *History and Society*, Calcutta, 1976, pp. 15-23.

15

TEXT BOOKS

In a civilized nation there will be always search for truth and criticism, which should be taken positively and constructively from the other side. In United States, a big book has been written by James W. Loewen entitled *"Lies My Teacher Told Me"*[1] which is the National Bestseller. Howard Zinn, author of *"A People's History of the United States"* has recommended that "Every Teacher, every student of history, every citizen should read this book (By W. Loewen). It is both a refreshing antidote to what has passed for history in our educational system and a one volume education in itself."

REFERENCE

1. James W. Loewen, *Lies My Teacher Told Me*, Everything Your American History Textbook Got Wrong, Published by Simon & Schuster, New York, 1955, First Touchstone Edition, USA, 1996, pp. 1-377.

16

AMERICAN HISTORIOGRAPHY DURING THE NINETEENTH AND THE TWENTIETH CENTURIES

The history writing in America was affected by the complex of ideas labelled Darwinism and the related belief that history is or should be a science which was clearly an offshoot of Positivism which had affected the whole of Europe during the nineteenth century.[1] By the last quarter of the nineteenth century historical scholarship became a profession which till then had been the avocation of lawyers, clergy or businessmen. In 1880 there were only eleven professors of history in the United States. In the America Nation series, which appeared between 1904 and 1907, twenty-one of the twenty-four authors were university professors. Herbert B. Adams worked for formation of the American Historical Association in 1884 and conducted its affairs for many years afterwards. Adams produced his two volume life and writing of Jared Sparks (Boston, 1893) which he wrote at the request of the Sparks family.[2]

By the end of the nineteenth century a large and rapidly expanding group of University professors of history in the United States emerged who had established a professional historical organization with a professional journal and showed commendable zeal in advancing the interests both of the profession and of scholarship. It was a general belief shared by American scholars that history is a science. Science had triumphed in the thought of the nineteenth century and this may be called an effect of positivism, which prevailed throughout Europe in the nineteenth century so much so even a new church took the name "Christian Science". Biology was the science to which the historians had frequently turned; its terminology they frequently used in historical writing. "The significance of the Frontier in American History", by Frederick Jackson Turner in

1893 was an application of Darwinism to history. The new seminary method of training scholars, was according to a typical statement, "essentially the methods of biology applied to history".[3]

It was over and again emphasised that the claim of history as a science is founded in the fact that it has a scientific method.[4] For this group of historians, the great figure was not the English scientist, Darwin, but the German historian, Von Ranke. Through the influence of the students of "this father of historical science" the historical seminary was extended throughout Germany and the world. It was Henry Adams who empahsised, "should history ever become a true science, it must expect to establish its laws..."[5] To formulate the laws of history was, he believed, the great challenge to the historians of the period. At another extreme this meaning of scientific history was explained as has been suggested by the natural sciences, was the belief that scientific history consisted of a search for facts alone, with no laws or generalizations and with a renunciation of all philosophy. Rhodes stated that since the object of the historian "is to tell a story and leave philosophy to others", his aim had been "to get rid so far as possible of all preconceived notions and theories". Another version was that to be scientific was to be objective. To be objective was to study critically the genuine sources, and subsequently to describe impartially the facts of history with the same detached mind and in the same manner which, it was believed, other scientists regarded natural phenomena. The facts, thus scientifically established without benefit of hypothesis or of generalization, would "speak for themselves". Interruptions by the historian were not regarded with favour. Scientific historian need not concern himself with more than the establishment of the facts.[6] The American historians tried to emulate Von Ranke's scientific history after 1875, that the chief duty of the historian was to establish *wie es eigentlich gewesen* ...The field of the historian is, and must long remain, the discovery and recording of what actually happened."[7]

After the turn of the century a number of American scholars began to undermine the prevailing theory. It was only in 1935, that an American stated fully the elements and assumptions of the faith in objective scientific history. The first is that the facts of history have existed as an object or series of objects outside the mind of historian. The second is that the historian can know this object or series of objects and can describe it as it objectively existed. This involves the question of documentation, the only way in which a historian can observe the facts. But documentation can only cover a small fraction of the events of history. This also requires the historian to divest himself all philosophical, religious, political, economic, social, sex, moral and aesthetic interests so that he can view the facts with strict impartiality. It also presupposes that the facts can be grasped by a purely rational or intellectual process can grasp the facts. A final major assumption is that the facts of history have some structural organization through inner, perhaps causal, relations, which any impartial historian can ascertain and on which all must agree.

The challenging of these assumptions has raised the most crucial problem confronting contemporary historiography in all it branches. If the challenge is not successfully met, the period of "scientific history" in America will be definitely ended. The challenge itself is, in the main, the application to the business of the historiographer of preconceptions, which are primarily philosophical and psychological in their context and origins, and about which no generally accepted verdict can as yet be said to have been rendered. Hence there is need of modification of current conceptions of "scientific history" and as the historians are compelled to consider the nature of the foundations on which their historical constructions rest, a more sophisticated scholarship must inevitably result.[8]

Historical Scholarship in the Twentieth Century

Historical scholarship is inevitably integrated with the society of which it is a part. The nexus is economic as well ideological. Scholarly activity depends on the support, which its nourishing society can or will give it. Consequently, the first factor to record in consideration of historical scholarship is the first half of the twentieth century is that the United States during these fifty years has gone through an amazing economic development. It has amassed wealth unequalled by any other people during the same or any other period. Naturally scholarship in all fields has been affected by this development. There was a vast increase in library resources available in 1950 as compared to 1900. Other benefits came from private philanthropy, which that wealth made it possible. There are the grants-in-aid, the fellowships and the various subsidies which are now available and which were almost non-existent in 1900. At present there are approximately 7,500 professional historians, the vast majority of whom are teachers of history. The professional training of such numbers has been possible only because a considerable number of American colleges became universities where graduate work was offered and where scholarly attainments, especially in research, were the criticism for appointments and promotions. In fact, there is probably greater weight attached to research now than there was fifty years ago. The science of history has been successfully transplanted from its European source. "There has been great activity, specialization, elaborate organization, a much higher level of technical scholarly standards, a few distinctive schools of interpretation, and a growing interest in basic conceptions."[9] There are 86 journals under History since 1945. In addition we may name the *Journal of the History of Ideas* under philosophy and the *Journal of Economic History* under Economics.

In nearly everyone of the American States there is a historical society which publishes a journal. To win prestige and scholarly reputation, the editing of documents and similar brick piling activities conformed to the prevailing canons of the profession. The specialization and rigorous standards of scholarship brought significant changes in the form of the history written. Too many monographs have revealed superior scholarly abilities being wasted on inferior and insignificant subjects. One result of the adoption of the monograph as the vehicle for scholarly work has been the development of cooperative histories. The success, both scholarly and commercially, of the 26 volume American Nation Series of 1904-1907 encouraged other attempts. The most notable have been the *Yale Chronicles of America* (50 volumes), *The History of American Life* (13 volumes), *The Rise of Modern Europe* (20 volumes in progress), *A History of the South* (10 volumes in progress), *The Economic*

History of the United States (9 volumes in progress). Sometimes the cooperative work results from the combination of separate articles by different authors in the various volumes. Such as for example Tenny Frank's *Economic Survey of the Roman Empire*, the five volumes of which contain sections written by various American and European scholars. Such also as the ten-volume work, *The American Secretaries of State and their Diplomacy*, edited by S.F. Bemis and written by thirty-nine American scholars.

These attempts to supply histories on large themes while retaining the advantages of the monographs by specialists have not been attended by notable success. The standards of intensive research have usually been preserved in the separate parts of volumes, but the total picture has lacked unity, coherence, and proposition. "Apparently in historical work the best results can be obtained only when one mind studies all the data and erects the entire structure. Perhaps this is saying that the writing of history as in some respects a work of art and like a symphony must be creation of one man certainly the history of historical writing both in Europe and America shows no cooperative work equal to the achievements of individuals. The separate monographs may each be a scholarly jewel but when they are put together the resulting mosaic is a disappointing or drab affair."[10]

Since ventures of this size are expansive, they have been usually devoted to the History of the United States, as that as the field of history most likely to be bought by the American public.[11] Historians at no time created and used a specialized or technical terminology. The writing of textbooks loomed large among the activities of the professional scholars. Since there were a vast number of university students to buy them, the rewards for the author of a successful book have been large both in money and in prestige. Professional scholars usually subscribe to some theory or make some assumptions of the nature and limits of historiography, which determine the character of the history written. The American historians were silent about what they were doing but undoubtedly subscribed to the belief that history is a science. They did not establish any laws or generalizations and no history was written under the influence of this conception. For them scientific history meant the search for objective facts, which well, speak for themselves. This raged a controversy about scientific history and they turned to new faith, which is called historical relativism. Then the idea of progress influenced the thinking of near all Americans, which included the historians. As the twentieth century advanced belief in progress became difficult to maintain and was increasingly rare in historical writing. Among other ideas, which influenced historical scholarship, have been nationalism, liberalism, pragmatism, democracy, capitalism and the belief that man is primarily a rational being. Some psychologists, notably Freud, had already begun to stress the role of unconscious and the irrational. It only meant that the twentieth century American often thought in new terms. During the next fifty years American history became the most diligently cultivated field of scholarly activity.[12] A list of dissertations in progress in September 1949 published by the American Historical Association showed that 894 of a total of 1,634 were on the history be taught which was compiled by American scholars. Since 1920 more and more attention has been paid to the recent period in Europe, America and Asia. More emphasis was laid on political history, which included social and economic history. The history of international relations has been emphasized compared to the practice of the nineteenth century. The relative neglect of military history ended with World War II. The result has been a greatly increased amount of scholarly, though official, military history. In the twentieth century economic facts became an end in themselves. An increasing amount of attention was devoted to other human activities, to thought, to amusements, to eating, to science, to religion, all frequently thrown together under the label "Social History" which was claimed and denied as "The New History". The Americans did not subscribe to any single school of historical interpretation. Though some emphasis was laid on the economic interpretation of history, there have been very few American scholars who have enjoyed a strict Marxism economic determinism. The first starting and successful application of this school to American history was Charles A. Bread's *An Economic Interpretation of the Constitution*, which appeared in 1913. From then on economic interpretation flourished until towards the middle of the century more and more scholars repudiated it as a single explanation and insisted other forces and factors must also be taken into account.[13] The other schools of historical interpretation which deserve mention are "The Imperial School of Colonial History" and urban movement as a decisive factor in all phases of post-civil war. American history as the frontier and the Westward movement had been earlier.[14] Finally, we may say that "History is concerned with life, and he who works to understand or interpret human activity must himself have participated in affairs and the richer the experience, the better."[15]

REFERENCES

1. T.R. Sharma, *History of Historical Writing*, Part I, pp. 120ff.
2. W. Stull Holt, *Historical Scholarship in the United States and Other Essays*, University of Washington Press, Seattle and London, 1967, pp. 3-14.
3. *Ibid.* pp. 16-17.
4. *Ibid.* p.19.
5. *Ibid.* p.21.
6. *Ibid.* pp. 22-23.
7. *Ibid.* p.25; George Burton Adams, "History and the Philosophy of History", *American Historical Review* (January 1909), XIV, 236 as quoted.
8. W. Stull Holt, *op.cit.* p.28, Also see H.Hale Bellot, *American History and American Historians*, University of London, 1952, pp. 16-23.
9. W. Stull Holt, *op.cit.*, p.35.
10. W. Stull Holt, *op.cit.*, pp. 39-40.
11. *Ibid.* p.39.
12. *Ibid.* pp. 43-50.
13. *Ibid.* p.60.
14. H. Hale Bellot, *American History and American Historians*, The University of London, Great Britain, 1952.
15. W. Stull Holt, *op.cit.* p. 63.

17

COMMUNAL APPROACH TO HISTORY

India is a plural and multi-cultural society. It has a heritage of an ancient civilization and can draw from its hoary past good traditions and ideas as compared to some European nations, which made a recent beginning.

Actually communalistic approach is a distortion of history. It is against the nature of history, which has a holistic approach rather than being sectional, sectoral or one-sided.

It may be noted that a seminar on "Communalism in India" was organized by *Social Scientist* for three days (29-31 March 1990) whose Report is published in its June-July 1990 issue.[1] Various scholars expressed their divergent views and there could not be any consensus. The scholars pointed out the uneasy relationship between popular remembrance and historian's history. However they divided the period prior to 1947 and since 1947 as well as the kind of communalism, both of which are not appreciable in the secular fabric of the country. Among the features drawn from the past, which went into making of a religious community, writes Romila Thapar: "Among these an important component was the theory of the Aryan race. The theory gained popularity in mid-nineteenth century Europe, and was readily applied to India whenever the sources mentioned *aryas*. Its application had a definitive impact because it was argued that there was a racial segregation, which was seen, as biological and therefore innate.[2] Though Aryan is no longer seen as a term referring to biological race.[3] We cannot deny that the evolution of society and culture has taken place from both the Aryan-speaking groups and others. Further James Mill who in his History of British India periodised Indian history in terms of the Hindu civilization, the Muslim civilization and the British period. It was based on a very superficial knowledge of Indian history which divided Indian history into the Hindu, Muslim and British periods. Moreover historians never seriously questioned it until recently Marxist historians argued that it was both incorrect and inadequate. Nationalist historians earlier foreseeing the communal bias in it tried to change the nomenclature to Ancient, Medieval and Modern India, borrowing it from European history, without clarifying why a certain period ends and a new one begins. "Thus the Ancient period ended with the coming of the Muslims and the Medieval period with the coming of the British."[4]

There cannot be any solution to communalism, which is biased on feeling and thinking which can be changed by a healthy tradition borrowed from our ancient past, which stated *"Sarvam Khalu idam Braham"* (Everything emanates from god). And also *"Vasudhaiva Kutumbakam"* (The whole world is one family). The same idea is impregnated in the Vedic saying *"Sarvam Vishwamaekam Nidam"* (The whole world is one nest). A saying also goes "Love begets love". Let us love each other and not hate each other. We should think positively what we could do for each other rather than against each other as religion rather than against each other as religion never breeds hatred it preaches love. In Iqbal's words: *"Mazhab Nahin Sikhata Apas Mein Vaira Rakhna, Farishte se Behtar Hain Insan Banana, Magar Ismain Lagati Hai Mehnat Ziada"* (Religion never preaches mutual hatred. It is better to be good person than be an angel but it takes more work to be able to do so).

REFERENCES

1. Seminar on "Communalism in India": *A Report Social Scientist*, Vol.18, nos. 6-7, June-July, 1990, pp. 49-72.
2. *Ibid.* p.7.
3. *Ibid.;* Thomas R. Trautmann, *Aryans and British India*, New Delhi, 1997, *passim.* Also see Devahuti (ed.) *Problems of Indian Historiography*, Delhi, 1979, *passim*;
   Devahuti (ed.) *Bias in Indian Historiography*, Delhi, 1980, *passim.*
4. *Ibid.* p.6.

18

LOCAL AND REGIONAL APPROACH TO HISTORY

The appeal of a local history is universal and local historians can be found worldwide. In some places they practice independently while in others a district or the state takes an active role in supporting local history activities. The local history can be illuminating, the case is exemplified in United States of America.[1]

In Norway, to keep researchers informed about local history, and to connect them with new historical advances, there is a Norwegian Local Studies Journal.[2]

In Finland local history is related to home-district work. Here it is combined with ethnology, the development of communities, and ecological studies, and it is practiced in Finland districts. There is a more activist and comprehensive approach to local history than that taken by most historical societies in the United States. Local history can also be found throughout the Orient. In Japan, local histories are usually chronicles commissioned by a village major or official ... A Japanese local history can be a vast understanding, beginning with a discussion of the geology of the area, a description of the pre-historic peoples who inhabited which is now the village, and narrative of events and changes that have occurred there.[3]

Local histories are also popular in China... Much of the early Chinese local history had its origin in geographical studies and maps, defining and maintaining territory in ancient China was a necessary occupation... There is now a society of Chinese local history and chronicles to oversee the activities of local historians. A local chronicle is an "encyclopedia of place". The society issues a journal, entitled: *News Bulletin of Chinese Local History and Chronicles* and it encourages the education of its members.[4] In England, there have been a number of efforts on behalf of local history. Leicester University established a chair of

English Local History in 1952. Members of Leicester history department have written so many local studies, or by people who have studied there, that in 1982 the University issued a bibliography listing all such works that can be associated with that school.[5]

In United States major credit for a renewal of interest in local history goes to the Bicentennial celebration of the mid-1970s, for it continued this decentralizing trend by dividing the American experience into its varied parts... Nevertheless the Americans were urged to write the history of America's hometowns.[6]

Attributes of a Local Historian

(1) A local historian researches, collects, preserves and communicates what he or she knows.

(2) Another major aspect is reading which does not mean reading for research, which is taken for granted. He is expected to read widely for general historical knowledge for new approaches to material, and for insights into human behaviour.

(3) He should look at a wide range of local and academic histories in order to judge how best to tell the story of the place where he lives. Reading also helps to understand state and regional variations which then can be tested in a local setting: while regions may have common attitudes and a shared history within a region, a great deal of variation can be found.[7] Marc Bloch wrote that "he frankly mistrusted the historian, who has no inclination to observe the men, the things, or the events around him for such a person will become only a useful antiquarian. Our local historian wants to be more than that, and contemporary knowledge informs our understanding of the past."

(4) A local historian needs imagination. Theodore Zeldin has written that: "imagination is ... as important to historians as new documents ... A local historian can do research and sit down to write a history or an article, but if he or she does not apply imagination to the material at

hand, the result is faint. Without the use of our imagination, paired with contemporary knowledge, we fail to ask ancillary questions or to seek other causes that would illuminate what we want to know."[8]

Regional History

The old trend in history for generalization of the basis of scanty information of any region has totally changed now. Apart from national history the focus is on region. It is quite obvious from the two volumes published on the *Cambridge Economic History of India*, Volume I, c 1200 – c 1750[9] and volume II, c.1757 – c. 1970, where the in information is given themewise and region-wise.

There is now abundance of material available on regional history not only based on regional literary sources but also the Government of India has well-established Archives in each region. In many parts of the country regional history is being taught as an important segment of the history syllabus. So it merits the attention not only of the specialist in the region but also of historians working on other aspects of Indian history.

"The initial interest in India in regional history grew out of the nationalist historical writing. It was motivated to some extent by a search for new source materials, a search which has resulted in an abundance of sources – archaeological, epigraphic, historical literature,, religious literature, archival records and family papers – all of which have added to the body of information available on the history of many regions of the sub-continent."[10]

The historical interest in regions such as South India, Bengal and Maharashtra has helped us to supplement the information from the records available outside the region. The spread of nationalism into various states increased the interest in regional history. In contemporary historical writing, there is a tendency of equating the present-day state boundary as boundary of the region holding it viable for all periods of history. Secondly, certain theories current in earlier historical writing, and believed to be almost automatic are endorsed even for regional history. Thirdly, there is search for a golden age though it always remained subjective. Research in regional history debates on historical assumptions at national level for an analysis of the historical patterns of the region. It tried to relate these patterns to the generalizations of Indian history, which helped the generalizations to be made at the wider level.

Romila Thapar further points to that we should care to know at what point of time the region got its identity as a region and having a history. Then we should consider the geographical boundaries of the region. We have to notice also when the larger frontiers coincided and sub-regions started interaction and relationship with each other, which forms a major part of historical research. We need to deeply deliberate over the data available to us to study the prosperity, migrations, invasions, trade routes, technology and religion affecting the importance or decay of a region. "In terms of comparative studies mention is often made of the kingdoms of the Punjab and the Marathas. They are said to have been motivated by an anti-Muslim sentiment which helped them to be rid of central, imperial authority ... There are examples in history of Maharashtra which is equated with the rise of the Maratha kingdom, that of Rajasthan with the emergence of Mewar and Marwar, that of the Punjab with Sikhism and that of Tamil Nadu with Sangam literature... Historical events are not isolated phenomena, suspended in space and time and the historical matrix in which they are embodied is as important as the events."[11]

REFERENCES

1. Carol Kamman, *On Doing Local History* Reflections on What Local Historians do, Why and What it Means, *The American Association for State and Local History*, Nashville, Tennessee, 1986, Second printing, 1988, p.167.
2. *Ibid.* pp. 167-168.
3. *Ibid.* p.168.
4. *Ibid.* pp. 169-170.
5. *Ibid.* p. 170.
6. *Ibid.* p.173.
7. *Ibid.* pp. 120-121.
8. *Ibid.* p.122.
9. Dharma Kumar and Tapan Raychaudhari (eds.) *The Cambridge Economic History of India*, Vol. I, c 1200 – c. 1750, CUP, 1982, Reprinted 1984 and

Dharma Kumar (ed.) *The Cambridge Economic History of India* c.1757 – c. 1970, CUP, 1982, Reprinted 1984.

10. Romila Thapar, *Ancient Indian Social History*, New Delhi, 1979, p. 361.
11. *Ibid.* pp. 375-376.

19

HISTORIOPHOTY

The growth of cinema and television has produced a mixture of sight and sound that the media may be used for imagery and interpretation of human events. We have quoted earlier the work of Norman K. Denizin wherein the Part I of the book deals with the Post-modernism and the Part II deals with 'Learning from Cinema'.[1] The post-modernism erases all boundaries between the past and the present, identification with the real and representative, a codification of sexuality and desire, a pornography of the visible and it covers intense emotional experiences shaped by anxiety, alienation, resentment and a detachment from others.[2] It works on words, texts and meanings which play a pivotal role in the decisive performances of race, class and gender relations that shape the emergent political conditions in the post-modern world. The popular culture of the past, especially film and pop music define the present.[3] This system combines the First and Third Worlds and articulates a set of ideologies, which value family, sexuality, work and leisure.[4]

Sohrab M. Modi talks about historical and biographical films, which can be stated as pages torn from history. He cites the examples of filmmaking of *Pukar*, a patriotic film, *Sikander* that dealt with Alexander's invasion of India, *Prithvi Vallabh*, *Ek-Din-Ka-Sultan*, *Jhansi Ki Rani* and *Mirza Ghalib*.

Modi further elaborates on this highly specialized branch of filmmaking that any undue tampering with the original subject or any attempt to create a half-way house in order to ensure success at the box office not only defeats its own purpose but is seldom rewarded on any count.[5] A biographer or a historian may err if he is not having the proper grasp of his subject. So also a producer is quite liable to commit lapses and breaches in undertaking a film biography or a historical film. The most crucial question is that of 'cinematic licence' which a producer or director has to exercise in transcribing the subject from the book to the screen. Modi remarks: "This has always been a controversial point, and opinions differ as to how far a producer can take liberties with a biography or with history and to what degree he should be faithful to the original."[6] Though Modi himself admits that no film is ever complete or effective without a proper fusion of fact or fiction, that a motion picture being a live-action medium has to fulfil its primary aim of entertainment which it fails to do if it were merely to revive documentary evidence or else provide illustrations for the history textbooks in a dull, unromantic, unimaginative or prosaic fashion. About historical accuracy of the film of Henry VIII produced by Alexander Korda, Modi cites the example of one character of the film, namely Anne of Cleves, who bore any recognizable resemblance to the original. The criticism was so fantastic that Korda had to declare "there is nothing more futile than to attempt to satisfy the painstaking exactitude of the expert."[7] Similarly Modi in his biographical film *Mirza Ghalib*, quotes his experience when a section of the Urdu press given to sensationalism raised a controversy as to whether Ghalib sported a beard or not. But more important than the facial resemblance to the original characters as conceived or misconceived through legends and their portrayals on the screen is the spirit of the character and the general atmosphere of the period covered. Moreover you need full cooperation from the state for making a historical and biographical film. Modi cites an example in America where all the available resources of the Army, the Navy and the Air Force are placed at the disposal of a producer who makes facilities for an ambitious film.[8] He expresses his desire to Government of India to follow suit to encourage dramatizing our history. A film of the magnitude of *Jhansi Ki Rani*, for example, the producer needs full support and cooperation from army authorities for the purposes of authenticity and spectacular effects in the battle sequences.[9] The thrill of making good pictures comes all the greater when one is really inspired by the subject, when the creative urge is uppermost and overwhelming and the path is completely free from distractions.

Modi states that in India percentage of historical and biographical films is not very high whereas the percentage of love stories and mythologicals showed a remarkably consistent average. He quotes Dr. Radhakrishnan who once said thus about films: "We are getting too much of this mythology. We should retain all our ancient ideals but they must find parallels in the life of modern people and modern conditions. The industry must give to the nation pictures around our daily life and its social and economic problems. India's history, both medieval and modern, will supply any number of themes for biographical pictures, travelogues, documentaries, newsreels and shorts such as they produce in America must now be started here."[10]

P.K. Atri another participant in the symposium quotes (from Lenin), "Of all the arts, the most important is that of the Cinema". It is free from the limitation of time and space. He quotes some biographical films such as *Sikander, Chhatrapati Shivaji, Vidyapati, Tukaram* and *Gyaneshwar*. All history cannot be rendered on the screen. It has to be carefully censored and winnowed. Historical incidents have to be properly evaluated and projected in reality.[11]

Another participant Dr. Kalidas Nag suggests filmmaking on the "dawn of Indian Civilization", historical films on the Vedic and Epic Ages, "Age of Rationalism and Reformation" and certain biographical films on heroic personalities.[12]

We know the historical films on *Gandhi*, *Anarkali* and Ashoka the Great created a great sensation among the viewers. It has been suggested that the historians in collaboration with the filmmakers should evolve a research methodology or production of films or documentaries. It is probable that some fictional elements may change the texture of the filmmaking it unhistorical. It is agreed upon that any film can be a mixture of fact and fiction. Hence there is an urgent need to produce literature and establish associations of scholars of both history and cinema for arriving at an understanding and awareness of historical projects.[13] Seeing the complexity of filmmaking, presenting history on screen, analytical approaches, training in cinematography and understanding of communication theories require rigorous training.[14]

REFERENCES

1. Norman K. Denzin, *Images of Postmodern Society*, London, 1991, 1993 edition.
2. T.R. Sharma, *Research Methodology in History*, New Delhi, 2001, pp. 30-31.
3. *Ibid.* p.31.
4. *Ibid.* pp. 31-32.
5. *Ibid.*
6. *Historical and Biographical Films: A Symposium*, The Publications Division, Government of India, Delhi, 1956, p.7.
7. *Ibid.* p.7.
8. *Ibid.* p.8.
9. *Ibid.*
10. *Ibid.* p.9.
11. *Ibid.* pp. 10-13.
12. *Ibid.* p.15.
13. Bajaj, *op.cit.*, pp. 79-80.
14. *Ibid.* p.80.

BIBLIOGRAPHY

Abraham, M. Francis, *Modern Sociological Theory, An Introduction*, OUP, Fifth Impression, 2000.

Abraham, Francis, Morgan, John Henry, *Sociological Thought*, Madras, 1996.

Anand, Sugam. *Modern Indian Historiography*, Agra, 1991.

Bellot H. Hale, *American History and American Historians*, University of Oklahoma Press, Norman, 1952.

Brown, Donald, E., *Hierarchy, History & Human Nature*, The University of Arizona Press, Tricson, 1988.

Butterfield, H., *The Whig Interpretation of History*, New York, 1965.

Carr, E.H., *What is History?*, Penguin, England, 1965.

Cohen, G.A., *Karl Marx's Theory of History: A Defence*, Oxford, 1978.

Collingwood, R.G., *The Idea of History*, OUP, London, Reprinted, 1973.

Cullagh, Bahan Mc, *Justifying Historical Descriptions*, CUP, 1984.

Danaher Geoff, Schirato Tony *et al.*, *Understanding Foucault*, Delhi, 2001, 1st Indian edn.

Dray, William, *Perspectives on History*, London, 1980.

Darwin, C., *The Origin of Species,* VI edn., London, 1906.

Devahuti (ed.), *Bias in Indian Historiography*, Delhi, 1980.

Dube, S.C., *Anthropology, The Study of Man*, Hyderabad, 1952.

Elton, G.R., *The Practice of History*, London, 1967.

Elton, G.R., *Reformation Europe 1517-1559,* Fontana, 1978 edn.

Faruqi, N.A., *Early Muslim Historiography*, Delhi, 1979.

Finley, M.I., *The Use and Abuse of History*, London, 1975.

Fogel, Robert William & G.R. Elton, *Which Road to the Past?*, London, 1983.

Gardiner, Patrick (ed.), *The Philosophy of History*, OUP, 1974, reprinted 1984.

Gay, Peter, *Style in History*, New York, 1976.

Gooch, G.P., *History and Historians in the Nineteenth Century*, London, 1920.

Gottshalk, Louis, *Understanding History*, New York, 1968 edn.

Hall, Calvin. S. & Gardner Lindzey, *Theories of Personality*, New Delhi, 3rd edn., Reprinted, 1985.

Hasan, Mohibbul & Mujeeb, M. (eds.), *Historians of Medieval India*, New Delhi, 1968.

Hirst, Paul Q., *Marxism and Historical Writing*, London, 1985.

Holt, Stull W., Historical Scholarship in United States and other Essays, University of Washington Press, Seathe, 1966.

Hook, Sidney (ed.), *Essays in Social History and Philosophy of History*, Oxford, 1974.

Iggers, Georg G., *New Directions in European Historiography*, Methuen, 1985.

Kabir, Humanyun, *Lessons of Indian History*, University of Gauhati, 1961.

Kammen Carol, *On Doing Local History*, American Association for State and Local History, Nashville, Tennessee, 1986.

Kosambi, D.D., *An Introduction to the Study of Indian History*, Bombay, Revised Second Edition, 1975.

Kosambi, D.D., *The Culture and Civilization of Ancient India in Historical Outline*, Delhi, Second Reprint, 1975.

Kuper Adam & Kuper Jessica, *The Social Science Encyclopaedia*, London, 1985.

Landes, David S. & Charles Tilly (eds.), *History as Social Science*, Prentice-Hall, New Jersey, 1971.

Langer, William L. (ed), *A Survey of European Civilization*, Boston, 1958.

Loewen, James W., *Lies My Teacher Told Me*, New York, 1996.

Lunia, B.N., *Some Historians of Medieval India*, Agra, 1969.

Majumdar, D.N., *Races and Cultures of India*, Bombay, 1973.

Majumdar, R.C., *Historiography of Modern India*, Bombay, 1970.

Martin, Rex, *Historical Explanation*, Cornell University, 1977.

Marwick, Arthur, *The Nature of History*, London, 1976 edn.

McCullagh, C. Bahan, *The Truth of History*, London, 1998.

Monier, Williams, *A Sanskrit-English Dictionary,* Delhi, 1963.

Mukhia, Harbans, *Historians and Historiography During the Reign of Akbar*, New Delhi, 1976.

Mukhopadhyay, S.K., *Evolution of Historiography in Modern India: 1900-1960*, Calcutta, 1981.

Narayanan, M.G.S., *Foundations of South Indian Society and Culture*, Delhi, 1994.

Nugent, T.K.Walter, *Creative History*, USA, 1967.

Pande, G.C., *Itihasa Swarup Evam Siddhanta* (in Hindi), Jaipur, 1973.

Pandey, Janak (ed.), *Social Reality*, New Delhi, 1988.

Panikkar, K.M., *A Survey of Indian History*, Bombay, 1977.

Plumb, J.H., *The Death of the Past*, London, 1984.

Pearce, F.G., *The Struggle of Modern Man*, OUP, 1973 edn.

Philips, C.H. (ed.), *Historians of India, Pakistan and Ceylon*, OUP, 1967.

Puri, B.N., *A Study of Indian History*, Bombay, 1971.

Pusalkar, A.D., *Studies in the Epics and Puranas*, Bombay, 1955.

Rader, Melvin, *Marx's Interpretation of History*, OUP, 1979.

Radhakrishnan, S. (ed.), *The Cultural Heritage of India*, Calcutta, 1970 Reprinted.

Rapson, E.J. (ed.), *The Cambridge History of India, Vol. I, Ancient India*, Indian Reprint, Delhi, 1955.

Raychauduri, H.C., *Political History of Ancient India*, 7th edn., Calcutta, 1972.

Sarkar, Sumit, *Writing Social History*, OUP, 1998.

Sharma, T.R., *The Concept of History*, Delhi, 1987.

Sharma, T.R., *Research Methodology in History*, Concept Publishing Company: New Delhi, 2001.

Stern, Fritz, *The Variety of History*, London, Second edition, 1970.

Tawney, R.H., *Religion and the Rise of Capitalism*, Penguin, England, Reprinted 1980.

Thapar, Romila, *Interpreting Early India*, Delhi, OUP, 4th Impression, 1997.

Viorst, Milton, *The Great Documents of Western Civilization*, Philadelphia, 3rd edn. 1967.

Warder, A.K., *An Introduction to Indian Historiography*, Bombay, 1972.

Webster, C.B. John, *An Introduction to History*, Delhi, 1977.

Wiener, P. Philip (ed.), *Dictionary of the History of Ideas*, New York, 1973.

Wiener, P. Philip (ed.), *Perspectives in American History* – New Series Vol.3, 1986, Cambridge University Press.

INDEX